Praise for Elizabeth Grace Saunders and
DIVINE TIME MANAGEMENT

"Making God the priority in your life is the primary challenge for all people of faith—Saunders's new book DIVINE TIME MANAGEMENT is essential reading for making this goal a reality."

—Greg McKeown, *New York Times* bestselling author of *Essentialism*

"A powerful and original take on time management, rooted deep in theology, that will radically transform how you think about scheduling and productivity."

—Cal Newport, *Wall Street Journal* bestselling author of *Deep Work*

"As Christians, the Bible says we are colaborers with Christ, but what does it truly mean to live and labor alongside God? In DIVINE TIME MANAGEMENT Elizabeth Saunders shares sound biblical perspectives to put your faith to work. Read it and apply her practical exercises to elevate your trust, increase your awareness of His presence, and transform the way you live out the divine mission He has for you."

—Leary Gates, cohost, *BoldIdea* podcast, and founder of StrategicCEO

DIVINE
TIME
MANAGEMENT

DIVINE
TIME
MANAGEMENT

THE JOY OF TRUSTING
GOD'S LOVING PLANS FOR YOU

ELIZABETH GRACE
SAUNDERS

NEW YORK   NASHVILLE

FaithWords
Hachette Book Group
1290 Avenue of the Americas, New York, NY 10104
faithwords.com
twitter.com/faithwords

First Edition: November 2017

FaithWords is a division of Hachette Book Group, Inc. The FaithWords name and logo are trademarks of Hachette Book Group, Inc.

The publisher is not responsible for websites (or their content) that are not owned by the publisher.

The Hachette Speakers Bureau provides a wide range of authors for speaking events. To find out more, go to www.hachettespeakersbureau.com or call (866) 376-6591.

Unless otherwise noted Scriptures are taken from THE HOLY BIBLE, NEW INTERNATIONAL VERSION®, NIV® Copyright © 1973, 1978, 1984, 2011 by Biblica, Inc.® Used by permission. All rights reserved worldwide.

Scripture quotations marked (DRA) are taken from the Douay-Rheims 1899 American Edition of the John Murphy Company, Baltimore, MD. Accessed on www.BibleGateway.com. Public domain.

Scripture quotations marked (KJV) are taken from the King James Version. Accessed on www.BibleGateway.com. Public domain.

Scripture quotations marked (KJ21) are taken from the 21st Century King James Version®, copyright © 1994. Used by permission of Deuel Enterprises, Inc., Gary, SD 57237. All rights reserved.

Scripture quotations marked (MSG) are taken from The Message. Copyright © 1993, 1994, 1995, 1996, 2000, 2001, 2002. Used by permission of NavPress Publishing Group.

Scripture quotations marked (NASB) are taken from the NEW AMERICAN STANDARD BIBLE®, Copyright © 1960, 1962, 1963, 1968, 1971, 1972, 1973, 1975, 1977, 1995 by The Lockman Foundation. Used by permission.

Scripture quotations marked (NLT) are taken from the Holy Bible, New Living Translation, copyright © 1996, 2004, 2007 by Tyndale House Foundation. Used by permission of Tyndale House Publishers, Inc., Carol Stream, Illinois 60188. All rights reserved.

Library of Congress Control Number: 2017947090

ISBN: 978-1-4789-7436-9 (trade paperback), 978-1-4789-7435-2 (ebook)

Printed in the United States of America

LSC-C

10 9 8 7 6 5 4 3 2 1

Consecrated to God

Contents

■ SECTION THREE ■

ALIGNMENT WITH GOD

Letter to You

Greetings! I'm so excited that you picked up *Divine Time Management*!

I'm Elizabeth, the author of this book. And if you could see me right now, you'd notice my eyes sparkling and my dimples showing because I just can't hide my joy. I know that in the process of reading this book your life will be transformed and your relationship with God deepened. I can't wait to hear your testimonies of what God does!

Also, this book isn't just about sharing what I know as an internationally recognized time management expert and lifelong Christian. It's sharing a piece of me. By the end of it, I hope you'll consider us friends.

To get the most out of this book, you'll need to actually read it. (Shocking how that works!) Here are a few time management coaching tips to help you receive the maximum benefit out of our time together.

First off, think about when you will read. It might be a routine such as reading at lunch or right before bed. Or you may prefer to go through the book in longer stretches, like when it's a weekend day or you're on vacation. To help you remember, you may want to put this book or your e-book reading device on your bedside table or in another place where you're likely to see it at the time when you want to dive in.

Sometimes a little positive peer pressure can go a long way in keeping on track. Consider reading this book with a small group, accountability group, book club, friend, or your significant other. This will not only keep you accountable, but also can lead to good discussions. You can download a free small-group discussion guide at www.DivineTimeBook.com.

When you read this book, expect to become a better version of yourself as you commit to *applying* what you read and allow God to transform you. Think of this as a process where you celebrate consistently (not necessarily constantly) living in trust, love, and alignment with God. This is not about performance or being perfect. You will get off track sometimes, but God in His kindness and goodness will always grow you and reward you when you seek Him.

This book is written from my perspective as a Christian who has experience with a number of different churches and Christian groups and currently attends a nondenominational church. Please feel free to use what's helpful for you from this book based on your faith background, biblical understanding, and relationship with God.

Finally, if you want all my latest and greatest time investment tips, go to www.ScheduleMakeover.com, or to find out more about my other books, coaching, and speaking, visit www.Real LifeE.com. My first book, *The 3 Secrets to Effective Time Investment*, is a comprehensive look at lasting behavioral change with time management, and my second book, *How to Invest Your Time Like Money*, is a focused look at how to allocate your time to align with your priorities. Both offer a lot of practical tools and tips that can help you if you're looking for more tactical support in addition to the spiritual perspective covered in *Divine Time Management*.

My prayer is that through reading this book, you will not only see a transformation in your time management but also in your relationship with God, others, and yourself. It's time to experience the joy of trusting God's loving plans for you, so let's begin!

God's best,
Elizabeth

"For I know the plans I have for you," declares the LORD, *"plans to prosper you and not to harm you, plans to give you hope and a future."*

JEREMIAH 29:11

One thing I have desired of the LORD, that will I seek after;
That I may dwell in the house of the LORD all the days of my life,
To behold the beauty of the LORD, and to enquire in His temple.

PSALM 27:4 KJV

Preface

A story of transformation from a member of the Divine Time Management coaching group, in her own words:

At the start of Divine Time Management, I was at a point in my life where I didn't really know where to go or who to turn to. I had so many unanswered questions, confusion, and doubt. I lacked confidence in myself. I suffered days of feeling weary and mentally exhausted—trying to figure out and have control over every aspect of my life.

Through Divine Time Management, I have learned to let go and leave my path up to God. I have learned to let go of control and accept that God has chosen this path for me, and He will guide me every step of the way. I have learned how to better cope with my feelings of guilt, anxiety, and doubt through prayer.

In the past, I tried to search for peace, happiness, and answers through excessive exercise, in people, in my own head.

Now, I leave it up to God.

I praise and live for Him. He provides me with the ability to feel happiness and feel loved. Most importantly,

Divine Time Management has brought me closer to God, and that is an amazing thing.

Divine Time Management takes you through a wonderful journey, a journey that will touch your heart in more ways than others, and a journey and a life change you will never forget. The journey of: self-acceptance through God's Word, a journey of learning about forgiveness, a journey of practicing self-care, a journey of analyzing your life and your relationships, a journey of letting go of hurt you may have experienced at any moment in your life and still be holding on to.

Elizabeth has such a calming and positive voice. She speaks with words of kindness and wisdom through her readings and reflections from the Bible and other sources. She helps to heal you through prayer and shows compassion and kindness for whatever is going on in your life.

I have been able to finally find peace and feel at ease. I have learned to relax certain areas in my body that were tense due to fear. I used to hold fear and stress in my stomach, in my digestive system. I used to see the results of fear come out in my skin when I was stressed out. I have learned to acknowledge my fears and pray about them to overcome them.

I know how to calm myself now when I do feel anxious, and I have less days of being anxious or worried.

I have less moments of feeling guilty for doing things for myself and practicing self-care. I have less worry about what others think of me and less questioning what is going on in my life. I am more calm most days. I am so thankful to have had the opportunity to be a part of this wonderful journey with Elizabeth and friends.

Paige Waugh[1]

Isn't God amazing?

Whenever I have a conversation with someone about starting a time management coaching program, I always state clearly that this is a partnership. That I'm going to give 100 percent of what I've got but he or she also needs to give 100 percent. I'm not able or willing to rescue anyone or force anyone to do anything. Each person needs to fully commit to the process to achieve the desired results.

To get what you want out of this book, I encourage you to not only read but also be open to this material. Let it go from your head to your heart to your spirit. Ask God to show you what you need to read and what you then need to do. When you invite God into your process of change, this all becomes *divine time management*. That means you and I have a third partner in the process—God. He is omniscient, omnipotent, and a whole bunch of other amazing things. God can do more in an instant than we can do in a lifetime—and He does.

With God you can go from stressed to peaceful, anxious to confident, angry to joyful, and trapped to free literally within days. It simply takes a shift of heart from control to trust, love, and alignment with God.

Throughout this book, I will share about transformations in my own life and the lives of others. When you read them, I pray you

---

[1] Paige Waugh, e-mail to author, March 9, 2016.

will have hope—hope in the Lord and give all the praise and glory to Him. All healing comes from God and is for His glory and the good of the people who He loves and treasures, which includes you.

Welcome to the journey of *Divine Time Management*, one where we let go of fear-based control to be free to choose to invest our time in God's best.

In His grace,
Elizabeth

Israel, put your hope in the LORD,
for with the LORD *is unfailing love*
and with him is full redemption.

PSALM 130:7

■ ■ ■

TRUST IN GOD AT THE CENTER

CHAPTER 1

Control Is Not the Goal

Then the LORD said to Moses, "Go to Pharaoh and say to him,
'This is what the LORD, the God of the Hebrews, says: "Let my
people go, so that they may worship me." ' "

EXODUS 9:1

Q: What do you do when: you want to manage your time better but you don't want to be more self-disciplined? You don't want to try harder? You don't want to squeeze in more? You want to rest in God? You want to trust in Him to do the work? You want to enter into the peace, joy, and abundant life He promises?

A: Divine time management.

As a time management—or as I like to call it, "time investment"—expert since 2009, I've taught thousands of individuals how to align their time with their priorities through time management coaching and training. It's been incredibly fulfilling to see individuals' stress levels plummet and their achievement levels rise.

But in 2015, I had a crisis of faith. Not in the sense of losing faith—I've been a Christian for as long as I can remember, and my relationship with God is deeper than ever. But in the sense that I realized that although what I taught wasn't intrinsically bad, the heart of it had been off. In so many ways, I had aimed to create an approach to time management that eliminated the need for God by positioning faith as a nice accessory and putting individuals' ability to control themselves and their environments at the core.

In 2015, my time management expertise collided with my faith in God, and the concept of "divine time management" emerged. A concept that acknowledged the reality that I'm not meant to live my life by my own strength. I'm created to walk hand in hand with my heavenly daddy all of my days. So are you.

This integration resulted in a group coaching program as well as this book. *Divine Time Management* looks to redirect the aim of time management back to the appropriate target so people of faith can receive God's best.

Here's how the essence of divine time management began to unfold in my life shortly after I felt prompted by God to fully integrate my professional life with the divine...

Mid-September to mid-October of 2015 was nonstop. During that time, I had a huge influx of new client work, spoke at a conference, and flew back and forth between the eastern time zone and the Pacific time zone multiple times for personal and professional commitments. This led to my body having the not-so-brilliant idea to wake up just a few hours after I had fallen asleep when I was on the West Coast.

In the midst of it all, I tried to exercise regularly, keep in touch with friends, stay involved in my church, and serve my coaching clients.

For the majority of this crazy-busy month, I stayed calm and collected through applying the time investment techniques I have shared openly for years. I employed these basic principles of time management as if by default, since I was used to them allowing me to be "in control":

- **Focus on top work priorities:** I identified and tackled the most important tasks first. And I said no to or delayed everything else.
- **Maintain self-care:** Despite the intensity of my schedule, I refused the temptation to stay up working super late, keeping in mind that adequate sleep is necessary to being productive, calm, and happy. I also made time for physical activity—even if it was just a quick walk. Caring for your body is key to emotional and energy regulation.
- **Delegate:** I relied on the help of the absolutely wonderful people who assist with my business, like setting up new client appointments and bookkeeping, and recruited some help around the house with cleaning and grocery shopping.
- **Keep time for relationships:** Even when at my busiest, I made it a priority to spend time with God each morning and to be there for the people I care about, whether that meant having a good phone conversation or going to church.

Even though these techniques helped, during the final week of what felt like a monthlong sprint, I still hit a wall. It didn't matter that a more normal pace was imminent. The following week I would return to my less intense, personal healthy workload of forty to forty-five hours, with fewer calls scheduled. But telling myself that I simply had a few more days to go, that I needed to suck it up, to be grateful because many people have much harder lives than me, *just didn't cut it*. Something inside of me wanted to mutiny. It wanted to hide in my bed, close my eyes, and hope my day of back-to-back meetings would somehow magically disappear.

I was just so exhausted.

The frequent travel, the toll that being in different time zones had taken on my body, and the almost back-to-back personal and professional commitments had sapped all my energy and then some.

I was lying in bed thinking about the obligations that loomed over the course of the day. I realized that although my time management techniques had taken me far, they absolutely did not have the ability to carry me across the finish line. I had nothing left in me. My mind knew so much needed to get done, but my body felt like a lead anchor sunk into the depths of my mattress.

The only thing that brought comfort to my soul was crying out to God.

I cried out to let Him know that I was so tired. I just didn't want to do . . . anything.

Although I knew relief would come very soon, right there and right then, I just needed help to get through the day—and to do so with peace and joy.

And God answered.

I was painfully aware that some of my misestimation about my plans and my own capacity to handle them had led to the time being so intense. God let me know that I didn't need to feel guilty. He reassured me that it was OK to admit that I was really tired, that just because some people have it even harder than I do didn't invalidate my experience. He encouraged me to rest in Him and allow His strong-yet-sweet and gentle love carry me over the next few days.

From that place of humility and vulnerability, I was able to lean on the Lord's strength. God got me out of bed. God carried me through all of my meetings. God gave me the ability to complete the most important work. And God gifted me with the capacity to truly enjoy the end of that week, which included a weekend visit from my brother and parents.

I saw God come through—orchestrating my days more perfectly than I could ever have planned and giving me supernatural peace.

The reason I share this with you is that I want to give you the *whole truth* of how life actually works for me so that you know what to do when you come to the end of yourself and your own ability to manage your time. The week I just described is a perfect example of how my relationship with God and trust in Him are the true answers to my biggest time management challenges as well as to living a joyful, peaceful, and abundant life.

Yes, there's so much that can be done from a strictly practical time investment point of view. But especially as you begin to take on bigger and better things, you will come to the end of your human understanding and need God to guide you. At the end of yourself, I promise you will find that God is more than enough.

TURNING YOUR WORLD UPSIDE DOWN

This book is an opportunity to share what I've learned regarding God-centered time management and to encourage you on this journey. At first it made me feel vulnerable to begin to put on paper the truths that God had been revealing to me. You'll get an opportunity to witness some of my most poignant moments with the Lord—piles of Kleenex and all. But now, I'm just excited for as many people as possible to read this book and experience the same level of transformation I've had in writing it. It's been amazing! My hope is that these encounters help you more fully understand the heart of God.

You'll also hear some things that you've never heard before in traditional self-improvement books and maybe not even within the church. I know that may make some of you uncomfortable at first and maybe even a little bit sad when you realize that life didn't have to be as hard as you've made it. But my prayer is that through this book, you will gain greater freedom and joy from this day forward. Instead of staying in the past with regret, you can look to the future with hope.

> "Forget the former things;
> do not dwell on the past.
> See, I am doing a new thing!
> Now it springs up; do you not
> perceive it?
> I am making a way in the
> wilderness
> and streams in the
> wasteland."
> ISAIAH 43:18-19

The truth is, striving for self-empowerment actually results in disempowerment because it disconnects us from the source of our true strength—God. Trying to figure everything out and muscling through things ourselves produces bondage instead of freedom. That's why the very first step in divine time management is to start to partner with God in our time management.

For most people, even Christians, our first thought when we get up in the morning—or wake up in the middle of the night—is, "What do I need to do today?" And when we feel overwhelmed, the knee-jerk response can be, "How can I handle this situation?" But instead of jumping in and assuming we need to do everything on our own, a better approach is to ask: "God, what do you want me to do today?" When we feel overwhelmed, it's most effective to stop and ask: "God, what—if anything—do you want me to do about these circumstances?"

I encourage you to begin the habit of praying over your days instead of jumping in without checking in with the Big Guy. You can pray any way you would like, but here's a simple prayer to start:

> "Dear God, Good morning. Thank You for this new day and the opportunity to love and serve You and others. Please lead and guide my actions today. Make it clear what I should or should not do. And please allow me to live from a place of peace, rest, joy, and love in You. In Jesus' name. Amen."

When you start to feel overwhelmed or unsure, you can pray this prayer:

> "Dear God, I'm feeling overwhelmed and a bit anxious right now. I'm not sure what to do or not to do about this situation. Please lead and guide me on what is my part and what is Your part. Give me clarity on the next steps and help me to trust that everything will work out because You are actively at work on my behalf. You have the desire and capacity to take care of me and provide for me in this situation. Fill my heart with Your unshakable peace. In Jesus' name. Amen."

God is God. So we don't need to be.

Once you've taken the first step of partnering with God in

> *"Cease striving and know that I am God."*
> PSALM 46:10A NASB

your time management decisions, the next step is to make sure that you and God have the same aims in mind. It's hard to work effectively together as a team if you have disagreement on the location of the goal lines. But when we let go of the wrong goals and pursue the right goals, we get to be on the team of the best player in the whole wide world and can experience all the blessings He wants for us.

THE WRONG GOALS FOR TIME MANAGEMENT (THAT SEEM SO RIGHT)

I need to start out this section with a public apology. Because even though I've been a Christian for pretty much as long as I can remember, I'm not perfect. (Shocking—I know. But last time I checked there's only one Jesus.)

Given the fact that I'm human and have grown up in an imperfect world, I, like all of us, have picked up a whole bunch of worldly ways of thinking without even realizing it. Day by day, God is revealing truth to me and freeing me from wrong ways of thinking, hence this book.

It's exhilarating to realize how much easier, freer, and lighter life can be! I had a great life before. But as I pursue God's approach to time management more fully, it gets better and better and better. I get so excited about how much I'm learning and growing that I'm almost giddy when I share these truths with others. I know the pitch of my voice goes up.

But I do want to acknowledge that in the past I've promoted goals for time management that were not God's best, which we'll cover shortly.

I'm sorry. I didn't know better. I apologize for any ways in which I or other self-improvement experts may have led you astray from the truth of what God wanted for you. I know this book will take you a huge step forward in receiving God's best.

I also want to preface this discussion of the "wrong" goals for time management by noting that you need to understand the nuance of each area instead of looking at just one element. For example, we aren't supposed to try to control our lives, but a fruit of the Spirit is "self-control," so that is obviously something good and of God. I'm not insinuating that there should be no self-discipline, no practical time management practices, no pleasure in life, no achievement, or no conscious investment in relationships.

What I am pointing us toward in this section is that we must focus on God first, not on systems, tools, achievements, performance, or even a support network.

My heart's desire is that the Holy Spirit will show you how you can return to God wholeheartedly with how you invest your time. Not to make you feel bad, but because He loves you and wants you to have the best life possible!

You have complete freedom available to you in Christ through asking God's forgiveness and do not need to carry any false sense of guilt. If you've said you're sorry and turned back to God, it's done. By recognizing and repenting for these wrong goals for time management you can enter into the ease and joy that comes from alignment with God.

> *It is for freedom that Christ has set us free.*
> GALATIANS 5:1A

Wrong Goal: Control: I've Got This

Self-control, meaning an inner strength and mastery over your desires and passions,[2] is a virtue and a fruit of the Spirit (Gal. 5:22–23). But control, or having the perception that you can manage everyone and everything around you, is not something that God tells us to aim for in time management or in life in general. In fact, especially in regard to the future, God actively discourages us from believing that we are in control of our destiny.

The book of James reads:

> Come now, you who say, "Today or tomorrow we will go to such and such a city, and spend a year there and engage in business and make a profit." Yet you do not know what your life will be like tomorrow. You are just a vapor that appears for a little while and then vanishes away. Instead, you ought to say, "If the Lord wills, we will live and also do this or that." But as it is, you boast in your arrogance; all such boasting is evil.
>
> (James 4:13–16 NASB)

These verses shouldn't be interpreted to mean you should never plan anything, and sit on your couch eating potato chips expecting everything to come to you on a silver platter. As Proverbs 21:5 tell us: "The plans of the diligent lead to profit as surely as haste leads to poverty." Rather, the verses in James mean we should avoid thinking, "I've got this under control. I'm on top

---

[2] "Tu B'Shevat—The Fruit of the Spirit," Hebrew for Christians, accessed January 18, 2017, http://www.hebrew4christians.com/Holidays/Winter_Holi days/Tu_B_shevat/Fruit_Spirit/fruit_spirit.html.

of everything. I don't need God or anyone else." This attitude is about self-protection and self-provision instead of vulnerability to the Lord's goodness.

Time management should be approached diligently—with follow-through on what God has called you to do to the best of your abilities (see Prov. 12:27). But you should not put your trust in yourself or in your ability to organize or execute. One of the best indicators of where you have put your trust is how you react when your plans don't go as expected. If you become afraid or anxious, your trust most likely is in yourself or your plans. If you can stay calm and confident that everything will be OK, your trust most likely is in God.

Keep in mind that a struggle with perfectionist tendencies probably equates to a control issue.

As Brené Brown writes in her book *The Gifts of Imperfection*:

Perfectionism is the belief that if we live perfect, look perfect, and act perfect, we can minimize or avoid the pain of blame, judgment, and shame. It's a shield.... Perfectionism is, at its core, about trying to earn approval and acceptance. Most perfectionists were raised being praised for achievement and performance (grades, manners, rule-following, people-pleasing, appearance, sports). Somewhere along the way, we adopt this dangerous and debilitating belief system: I am what I accomplish and how well I accomplish it. *Please. Perform. Perfect.* Healthy striving is self-focused—*How can I improve?* Perfectionism is other-focused—*What will they think?*[3]

---

[3] Brené Brown, PhD, LMSW, *The Gifts of Imperfection: Let Go of Who You Think You're Supposed to Be and Embrace Who You Are* (Center City, MN: Hazelden, 2010), 56.

When you act like a perfectionist, you're trying to earn through control what you've already been freely given by God—unconditional love and acceptance (see Jer. 31:3). Perfectionism may make you feel strong and better than others on the surface—even justified in your judgment of others who can't "get it together."

But basing your security on your works—no matter how good they are—is self-righteousness and keeps you from all the freedom God wants for you in Christ. When you allow God to heal you of perfectionism in regards to time management, you allow yourself and others to enter into the rest God has for you.

The next time you "make a mistake," "overlook something," or "something doesn't go according to plan," keep calm and trust God.

Remind yourself: "I did my best." Then ask yourself, "Is there anything I need to do to make this situation right either by taking action or apologizing once?" Then ask yourself, "What can I learn for next time?" Once you've done what you can do and reflected on the lessons from the experience, give it to God and let it go.

Seriously.

No stressing. No going over again and again in your head how you did something wrong and you can't believe it. No profusely apologizing multiple times. No criticizing or making fun of yourself (in a bad way) later. Stop thinking and talking about it. And when a self-critical thought pops into your mind, use it as a trigger to remind yourself, "It's OK to be human, and God's got it covered."

REFLECTION QUESTIONS:

Have I pursued control as a goal in my life? If so, why?

RETURNING TO GOD:

God, I'm sorry for the ways in which I've sought to have total control of my life through time management techniques, routines, plans, or in other things like finances, appearance, or in maintaining the approval of others. I'm also sorry for how my quest for control has taken me away from all You have planned for me, and for how my actions may have negatively affected others. I ask for Your forgiveness and ask You to show me how to live my life free from the bondage of control by putting my trust in You instead of myself. In Jesus' name. Amen.

Wrong Goal: Pleasure: What Will Put Me at a 10?

Let's be honest. Pursuing pleasure just sounds soooo good.

Advertisers know this well. That's why whether it's describing the luscious taste of a dark chocolate ice cream bar filling your mouth with delight or the warm kiss of the sun caressing your body on white sandy beaches (when it's freezing cold where you live), they try to entice you by appealing to your desire for pleasure.

The same is true of marketing for most self-improvement products and services. They all promise basically the same thing, the "freedom" to indulge yourself in whatever you want, whenever you want it. They offer you "the life"—if you only buy into their brand.

But God's Word tells a different story:

> You do not have because you do not ask God. When you
> ask, you do not receive, because you ask with wrong

> motives, that you may spend what you get on your
> pleasures.... Don't you know that friendship with the
> world means enmity against God? Therefore, anyone
> who chooses to be a friend of the world becomes an
> enemy of God.
>
> (James 4:2b–4)

It's so easy to fall into the trap of trying to spend the most time experiencing the most pleasure possible.

At times, I've found myself trying to maximize enjoyment in my life by asking myself, when evaluating how to invest my time, "What would put me at a 10?"

But I've developed a strong conviction that it's the wrong question to be asking. It's not that I can't enjoy fun activities or that I shouldn't try to create a life where I have options of how to use my time. But when my focus is always on enhancing my experience of life, I am self-centered in my focus instead of God centered. This leads to forfeiting lasting satisfaction for fleeting pleasure.

I've discovered that in order to achieve true fulfillment, my ultimate goal needs to be to seek the kingdom of God and God's righteousness and trust that everything else will be added to me (see Matt. 6:33).

Not only is it solid biblical wisdom, but seeking a higher purpose than oneself simply is the only thing that produces lasting satisfaction.

Through my time management coaching programs, I have the opportunity to interact with people in a huge variety of life circumstances. Some of them have grown up very wealthy—think multiple homes in various parts of the world and sometimes even private planes. What they've told me based on their real-life experience of being able to fill their lives with "the most fun possible" or simply the ability "to do whatever they want," is that it really didn't make them happy. In some cases, it even made them depressed. Instead of constantly seeking pleasure, choosing to invest their time in meaningful activities like helping others not only gave them a true sense of purpose and satisfaction, but it also *intensified* their feelings of pleasure when they did engage in activities they found refreshing.

Seeking pleasure promises satisfaction but comes up short, because God wants us to seek Him first. The next time you find yourself intending to do something for a potentially excessive amount of time "just for fun," take a step back and ask God if this is the best investment of your time. For example, maybe you're planning on binging on Netflix. Watching a show or two is fine, but if you find yourself going into hours and hours, take a step back. Consider whether you might find a higher investment of your time in doing something nice for someone else, spending time with God, exercising, or finally moving ahead on a project that you've wanted to do for a long time.

REFLECTION QUESTIONS:
Is my main goal in life to spend as much time as possible chasing pleasure? What impact has that had on me?

RETURNING TO GOD:
God, I'm sorry for allowing myself to be drawn into focusing on pleasure as my first goal: for seeking first what feels good, what I think will make me happy, what allows me to escape, what gives me a high. You tell me not to make pleasure my aim,

but I've done it anyway. I ask Your forgiveness based on the finished work of the cross. I pray that You will help me to put my eyes on You, to want to obey You first, to put serving You and others above pleasing myself, and to trust that You will bless me with great, lasting joy as I do so. In Jesus' name. Amen.

■   ■   ■

Wrong Goal: Achievement: Getting Things Done

I know, I know. At this point, you're probably wondering, *What is Elizabeth thinking? What do you mean that achievement isn't supposed to be a goal for time management?! Isn't that what it's all about?*

Calm down—take a few deep breaths in through your nose, exhale through your mouth, and hang in there with me.

Yes, time management absolutely can and should help you to get things done. My first two books, *The 3 Secrets to Effective Time Investment* and *How to Invest Your Time Like Money*, go into a lot of practical strategies for doing just that.

Investing time in your priorities, following through on commitments, setting realistic expectations, and practicing good routines are all helpful. However, the ultimate goal of time management should not be achievement or getting things done. Instead, it should be about creating the freedom to do the Lord's will and in turn receive God's best. Just like when you have your finances in good order, you have more freedom to move and do what the Lord calls you to do. In the same way, when you have your time in order, you have more flexibility to use your time as God leads. That could sometimes mean being able to get more things done—like serving at church—but other times it could mean doing less, like spontaneously taking a day to have fun with a friend or family member or to simply rest in the Lord.

Achievements and getting things done are not bad in themselves. But it's problematic when you identify your self-worth in what you accomplish each day. When your worth becomes about your achievements, you feel great when you do great and awful when you "fail." Instead of receiving God's unconditional love, you turn life into a performance. Your identity should be in the fact that you're a child of God through accepting what Jesus accomplished in His life, death, and resurrection. His crowning achievement is enough.

It's also problematic when you use the need to "get work done" as a form of hiding. We'll explore false identities more in chapter 3. But it's worth noting here that sometimes we want to accomplish more tasks because checklists feel safer than relationships. If you're hiding behind your to-do list, ask God to help you to have the courage to start to peek out from behind your laptop enough to connect with Him and others.

And finally, relentlessly pursuing getting things done is the biggest issue when you become so fixated on finishing what you think you should be doing that you shut out the voice of God, which may be telling you to do something entirely different.

I may have done this, oh, once or twice (or many times!) before. So I'm still a work in progress in this area. But I'm learning.

It's hard to give up a way of being when it "feels so good" and you get a lot of kudos from people for it. But I believe it's worth it because God's ways are so much better. God says that He can do exceedingly, abundantly beyond what you can ask or think (see Eph. 3:20). So when you do what God wants, you get in on the best He has to offer.

* * *

I'd like to share with you two verses I've found really helpful to maintaining the right mind-set about achievement. When you find yourself starting to feel anxious about all you *have* to get done, I encourage you to read them. You may even want to print them out and have them in a place where you'll see them often, like pinned up in your workspace, taped to the back of a kitchen cupboard, or tucked in your Bible:

> This is what the Sovereign Lord, the Holy One of Israel, says: "In repentance and rest is your salvation, in quietness and trust is your strength."
>
> (Isaiah 30:15a)

> Unless the Lord builds the house,
> the builders labor in vain.
> Unless the Lord watches over the city,
> the guards stand watch in vain.
> In vain you rise early
> and stay up late,
> toiling for food to eat—
> for he grants sleep to those he loves.
>
> (Psalm 127:1–2)

REFLECTION QUESTIONS:

Is the main focus of my day completing as many tasks as possible or being in the Lord's will? Do I stop to ask God if He really wants me to do what I'm doing right now?

RETURNING TO GOD:

God, I'm sorry for focusing on using my time to get things done above all else—even You. I'm sorry for the ways in which I've worshipped my to-do list, being productive, having things in order, or simply being busy. I'm sorry for using achievement to make myself feel valuable, secure, and to define my place in the world. This has led me to put my goals above Your goals for my time. I'm also sorry for the ways in which I've used focusing on achieving things as a way to avoid being close to others and You. God, please help me to overcome my fear of intimacy and vulnerability with others and with You. I pray that You will fill me with the faith to trust You that I can rest, to trust You that I can stop constantly getting things done and everything will still be OK. I don't know how to be different, but I know You can change me, God. I open myself up to You for You to do Your healing work in me. In Jesus' most holy name. Amen.

Wrong Goal: Being the Super_____: Always Being There for People

I knew God wanted me to explore this topic as one of the wrong goals of time management. But I struggled a bit with exactly how to express it. Was the best way to describe it as "people-pleasing"? No, not really. "Relationships"? No, not that either.

Finally, I settled on "Being the Super_____" as the correct description of a wrong goal of time management. By that I mean always pushing yourself to meet impossibly high standards in a particular role without accounting for whether or not these standards are realistic, healthy, or aligned with God's best for you and others. When you're aiming to be the super_____, it may seem like you're killing yourself for others, but in reality you're pushing yourself beyond your max for your own sense of self-worth.

This wrong goal of time management is fairly subtle and really an issue of the heart. Two different people may be doing the same thing on the outside, but one may be aligned with God and the other misaligned.

When you're getting off track, you may think that you're doing the right thing because after loving God, loving others as ourselves is the second-greatest commandment (see Mark 12:28–31). But when your aim is to be the superdad, supermom, superfriend, super-churchgoer, superdaughter, or super-colleague, you're always there for people not because of your love for them but because you want to get affirmation and feel wanted and important.

It's a great thing to love people. It's an awesome thing to be there for people. And God wants us to serve others. But when you have a compulsion to "always be there," even going beyond what you can reasonably do without burning out, you're probably distracted from what God wants for you.

God doesn't ask you to be there for everyone. God asks you to be obedient and to do what He says to do, when He says to do it. Even Jesus couldn't always be there for people—even people He dearly loved—when they wanted Him to be there, such as in the story of Lazarus' death (see John 11:1–44). Yet God used the situation of Lazarus dying before Jesus' arrival to work an even greater miracle of raising Lazarus from the dead for God's glory.

If Jesus had tried to be a "superfriend" and rushed to Lazarus' home as soon as Mary and Martha asked Him to come, He would not have been in alignment with the Father and would not have fulfilled the full glory of God in the situation.

In the same way, if you're trying to be there for everyone all the time when God's not telling you to do so, you're not only going to tire yourself out, but you'll also diminish the glory of God in the situation. God is God for you, and God is God for others. He perfectly knows how to care for all His children.

The next time you find yourself about to volunteer to go above and beyond and beyond, pause before you commit. Think about why you are stretching yourself paper-thin: Are your motives purely to help or is this about being the "super" something? Are you coming from a place of faith or fear? Finally, is this something you sense is of God or of yourself? Then decide whether to move forward and take action or to keep your mouth shut. Often a moment of silence can spare you from weeks or months of stress.

When you choose to trust God enough to do only what He's calling you to do, you'll end up spending a lot less time *doing* and will see more positive results.

REFLECTION QUESTIONS:

Am I "there for people" more than God is telling me to be because I try to meet everyone's needs in my own strength? Do I ask God before volunteering to help with something, and am I sure other people actually want my help before I proceed?

RETURNING TO GOD:

God, I'm sorry for assuming that I always need to jump to people's aid without asking You, without knowing if You're calling me to help. I'm sorry for putting my worth in the fact that I can always be counted on, or in always being there for certain people. I am called to love people, but I'm not ultimately the source of all they need—You are. I'm sorry for people-pleasing and doing things that aren't right for me because I think they will make others happy. I repent for putting my security in my support system instead of in You. In Jesus' name, I pray You will help me to love others with a pure love—without an agenda. Please help me to trust You to provide for people when I'm not able to do so. Please show me how loved and cherished I am just for being me. In Jesus' name. Amen.

THE RIGHT AIM FOR DIVINE TIME MANAGEMENT

So now that we've explored some of the wrong goals for time management, it's time to turn our attention toward some of the right goals.

In the past, I took no strong public stand on what people's time investment priorities should be other than encouraging self-care, including time for relationships. I have respected, and do respect, people's right to decide what's important to them and to live their lives in alignment with their own values. My time coaching clients come from a vast array of life situations, cultural backgrounds, and religious beliefs. And I continue to work with and honor each person where they are on their journey.

But for those of you reading this book who are Christian, or at least curious about a Christian perspective, I want to share what I believe God has revealed to me about His goals for time management.

You can of course choose to accept or reject His ways. But as for me, I've found God's ways work best in the end even if they don't make sense in the beginning, so I highly recommend them.

In Matthew 22: 36–40, Jesus gives instruction on which commandments should be our focus:

> "Teacher, which is the greatest commandment in the Law?"
> Jesus replied: " 'Love the Lord your God with all your heart and with all your soul and with all your mind.' This is the first and greatest commandment.
> And the second is like it: 'Love your neighbor as yourself.'
> All the Law and the Prophets hang on these two commandments."

Jesus is the expert on how to live a life aligned with God, so His explanation of where to focus must be great advice. But if you're anything like me, you're probably wondering, "So what does this mean that I actually have to do?"

I'm sure millions of people have talked about the practical application of these verses, so I don't claim to have the exhaustive answer to that question. However, after spending a couple of years conversing with God on the topic, I came to the conclusion that there are three goals for time management that will best allow you to fulfill God's two greatest commandments, to love God and your neighbor and to live out His best for you. We'll fully unpack these in each of the three sections of this book. But in this chapter, we'll do a quick overview of what I believe are the three right goals for divine time management:

- Trust in God at the center
- Love for your true identity
- Alignment with God

We don't need to live in a self-reliant universe where we stress about doing everything right, and then pray to ask God to bless our plans. As children of the Most High God, we have the right to live in a God-centered universe. We can banish fear-based control. We can focus on love and alignment. And we can be free to choose God's best.

It's time to stop living below the line of our privilege.

Right Aim: Trust in God at the Center

There is a time and a place for building self-discipline, for wise decisions, and for effective tactics.

But all of these things should not be about us ensuring that our needs and wants are met through our own efforts. Instead, all of these strategies should free up our time so that we have enough space in our lives to love God, hear His voice, and stay connected with Him. Then from that place of greater intimacy with God, we can know what He wants us to do and how to do it. We can also receive all of the blessings God has for us.

Focusing on trusting God with all of our time and time management decisions opens up space for prayer and for rest. When we genuinely seek His will, God typically asks us to do less than we think we need to do and to rely on Him more. This moves us from a place of pride around how great we are at managing our time, and from fear when something doesn't go as it "should" to a place of humble confidence in God that everything is working out for the best. And trust in God frees us up to love people enough to let go—sometimes meaning letting go of our schedules to be with them, and sometimes meaning letting go of a compulsion to help others that isn't from the Lord.

Putting trust in God at the center of your time management allows you to enter into God's best.

REFLECTION QUESTIONS:

Does my approach to time management come from a place of trust in myself (my ability to manage my calendar, my diligence at recording to-do items, my expertise in planning, and my focus in execution), or trust in God? If I'm primarily trusting in my own abilities and efforts and looking to God as an afterthought, what would need to shift for me to first and foremost rely on God to ensure my time and efforts are invested in the best way possible?

RETURNING TO GOD:

God, I'm sorry for trying to provide for myself by being productive and having everything in order. Please forgive me for not wanting to have to trust You, for not wanting to be reliant and dependent upon You. Please show me how much You love me, how much You can be trusted, and how I can start making more space in my schedule for closeness with You. I want to see You work to come through for me and meet all of my needs. In Jesus' name. Amen.

Right Aim: Love for Your True Identity

Loving your true identity may seem like an odd goal for time management and even counter to the two greatest commandments. But God has shown me again and again through His Word, through pastors, and through my own life that knowing and loving your true identity is one of the most essential goals of God-centered time management.

When you know your true identity, you don't spend countless hours, days, months, or literally years of your life doing things out of a false sense of self. For example, you can avoid working far more hours than is healthy because you're a "high performer," volunteering so much you're often in tears and overwhelmed because you're "so helpful," or procrastinating your life away on the Internet because you're "lazy."

If you're in Christ, then you're a child of God (see Gal. 3:26). There is nothing more true about you than that. God has also crafted you with unique talents, gifts, and a personality that is different than anyone else. He wants you to live out who you are authentically and wholly in the world. When you understand whose you are and who you are, then your time management choices can bring about God's best for you and free you to love God and love others well.

We'll discuss knowing and loving your true identity in greater detail in section 2, "Love for Your True Identity," of this book. But to start a powerful, yet simple way to tell if your actions align with your true identity is to pay attention to your body. There's a good probability that you have some repressed negative emotions around the situation if you experience these physical symptoms before, during, or after an activity: back pain, ulcers, asthma, tension headache, migraine headache, eczema, psoriasis, acne, hives, dizziness, or ringing in the ears.[4] In short, when you force yourself to do something that the "true you" doesn't really want to do, your body turns on a "check engine" light.

If you want to find out more, there's a book, *Healing Back Pain: The Mind-Body Connection* by John E. Sarno, MD, that goes into extensive medical evidence for this connection between physical symptoms and repressed negative emotions. Also, I've seen this connection to be true both in my coaching clients' lives and in my own life. I had a coaching client who knew for months that she needed to resign from a committee because it was keeping her from other activities that were aligned with her values and her true self. But she hesitated to resign out of a sense of duty. Finally she realized she had to leave the committee when she got vertigo immediately before the committee meeting that left as soon as she was done with the meeting. Her body was making this clear: *This activity is not right for you.*

I know that for me, skin rashes on my shoulders or upper back almost always have to do with my taking over responsibility. I'm literally taking on something that is not mine and is not me, and my body reacts in protest. When I let go of the emotional burden, the skin irritation goes away.

Take a moment to think about any recent times when you suddenly had a physical symptom come on. Then ask God to show you if that activity is out of alignment with your true identity. If it is, try to find a way to drop it or address your negative emotions around it. By committing yourself to being the true you, you can experience the most blessings and, as a bonus, the best health.

---

[4] John E. Sarno, MD, *Healing Back Pain: The Mind-Body Connection* (New York: Warner Books, 1991), 49.

REFLECTION QUESTIONS:

Do I define myself based on how God sees me or based on worldly identities? Are there any areas of my life where a false sense of identity may drive my choices?

RETURNING TO GOD:

God, I'm sorry for not understanding my identity in You. I ask Your forgiveness for choosing to live my life based on a false sense of who I am or who I think that I should be. Please help me to see myself the way that You see me and to live out of that true sense of self. I don't want to waste any more time not being me and miss out on the opportunities You've given me to reflect Your glory to the world. In Jesus' name. Amen.

Right Aim: Alignment with God

Putting trust in God at the center of your time management while knowing, loving, and living out your true identity will naturally put you in a better position to invest your time well. From this position of strength, you have the ability to choose to stay in alignment with God. Alignment means being in the Lord's will on a big-picture level and walking in faithful obedience to what you believe God wants you to do on a day-by-day basis.

Desire for alignment with God was one of the most important qualities of the great men and women of the Bible from Abraham to David to Esther to the disciples. I believe it is an essential goal of divine time management.

God desires that each one of His children in any and all life circumstances constantly seek Him. I believe this is so important to God because He loves us and is jealous for our time and attention. He doesn't like it when we put other people or things ahead of Him. Also, as the perfect parent, God truly knows what's best. It grieves His heart when we make poor choices, including with our time, and it delights Him when we reap blessings by doing what He said to do.

Given that Jesus said the greatest commandments revolved around loving God and loving our neighbor as ourselves, I believe that alignment with God centers on right relationship with God, with others, and with ourselves.

We'll dive in depth into what alignment with God looks and feels like in section 3, "Alignment with God," of this book. But one simple step to take right now is to quickly ask yourself: *Where do I feel a sense of disconnection?* It might involve a wall between you and God, a blockade between you and another person, perhaps a coworker, family member, or friend, or even a rejection of some part of yourself. Then ask God how you could go from a sense of disconnection to one of love and connection in that relationship. This could happen through forgiveness, letting go of judgment, or another shift of mind.

One of the truths God has taught me is that we can't have a wall up in one area of our lives without having a wall up in all areas of our lives. There's a time and place for healthy boundaries. I'm not suggesting that you need to literally reconnect with past people in your life, especially if the relationships were unhealthy. But emotionally and spiritually, you can get into alignment with God by choosing to live a life without barriers erected by fear. Instead you can choose to operate from a free, open place of love for God, others, and yourself.

When we manage our time in such a way that we can stay in tune with and engaged in relationships, cultivate them, and hear God's voice about what we should or should not do, then we can experience His very best for our lives.

REFLECTION QUESTIONS:

Do I seek God regarding what I should do with my time? If not, what's one way that I can remind myself to ask Him about His plans for my day?

RETURNING TO GOD:

God, I'm sorry for so often getting out of relationship with You, with others, or even with myself. Please forgive me for being so focused on my plans or what I think needs to get done that I forget that my life is not my own. Help me to want to hear Your voice, to pursue it daily, and to believe that loving obedience will bring the best results. God, I don't know how to be different. I don't know how to stay relational in the process of getting things done. Please show me how. In Jesus' name. Amen.

■ ■ ■

Reflection Exercise: **BEING CLAY**

> *"Woe to the one who quarrels with his Maker—*
> *An earthenware vessel among the vessels of earth!*
> *Will the clay say to the potter, 'What are you doing?'*
> *Or the thing you are making say, 'He has no hands'?"*
>
> ISAIAH 45:9 NASB

At first this could seem like a discouraging passage. Is God mad at me? Should I be afraid? The answer is you absolutely shouldn't be afraid of God in a terrified sort of way. God is light and in Him is no darkness at all (see 1 John 1:5). God is the perfect Father and He will never try to maliciously hurt His children.

However, God is God and we're not. So this is a reminder to "fear God" in a reverence-and-respect sort of way. How this relates to our time management is that we can waste a lot of time, energy, and mental space resisting what God is doing in our lives. This could be in regard to where we're living or not living, the people who are around us or not around us, or how we think things "should be" versus how they are.

Of course if there are things that we can change that aren't right, we should take action. But when we've done what we can and things are what they are, we will be much better off accepting life as it is, being grateful, and trusting that God is working everything for our good (see Rom. 8:28).

So I would like you to take these steps:

- Think about any areas of your life where you are quarreling with God. This again is not about areas where you can change but about the unchangeables in your life right now. This usually relates to what you expected versus what is.
- Then I want you to spend a few minutes thinking about God's majesty and power. Reading further in Isaiah 45 can help with this, or you can simply go outside and look at the vastness of the stars at night.
- Finally, the next time you notice yourself getting worked up and distracted by being upset about how things are versus how you would like them to be, say a breath prayer. It can be as simple as saying, "God, I trust You," or "God, I don't understand, but I know You are good." If that's not enough to shake the feeling, take a few minutes to journal your thoughts or process them through going on a walk or talking with a friend. God wants you to tell Him how you

feel; you don't need to fake it. But then He wants and needs you to come back to a place of respect for and trust in His ways so that you can have peace.

I pray God opens up your heart and mind to accept His plans and be the most blessed and productive in the flow of His Holy Spirit. It's time to let go of control and step into the light.

God's best,

Elizabeth

"It is I who made the earth, and created man upon it.
I stretched out the heavens with My hands
And I ordained all their host."

ISAIAH 45:12 NASB

CHAPTER 2

Learning to Trust God

But I trust in your unfailing love;
my heart rejoices in your salvation.

PSALM 13:5

By quantifiable standards, I think I've trusted God more than the average churchgoer. For example: I've quit jobs (without another source of income), started businesses, moved across the country, ended relationships, and have tithed since I had my very first babysitting job, simply because I felt God told me to do so.

But since mid-2015, God has called me to a much deeper quality of trust.

It involves not only listening for God's instructions and doing what He says, but also trusting Him to do the work, to make things happen, and to really believe that the safest place is under His hand. This has led me to have many more results with much less effort. This has happened in big ways, such as working fewer hours in my business out of obedience to God's instruction, while God simultaneously enabled my income to increase. And in smaller ways, such as spending less time trying to perfectly plan each day, while God perfectly orchestrates the daily details of my life such as spontaneous calls at the exact right moment.

Like the children of Israel looking to the pillar of cloud by day and the pillar of fire by night for direction, my sole focus has become being under the Lord's hand. If He says pursue something, I do. If He says don't do something, I don't. Typically how I hear God's voice is through spending time in prayer. Usually when I pray about a decision, I either experience peace in my gut that this is the right thing to do, or I experience a strong, deep internal resistance. My mind might be thinking of all kinds of reasons of why I should or shouldn't do something, but my inner knowing is saying no or yes.

I now seek God's instruction in making small choices like which e-mails to respond to and which social invites to accept, as well as in large decisions like which work projects I focus on and where I live. It's been a truly grand reversal.

In the past, I trusted God in a big-picture sense, like with which job to accept or where to move. But I found my day-to-day safety and security in my own victories, like "being on top of everything": organized, in control, pleasing, and successful.

Now, I find my safety and security in being under the Lord's protection, and in embracing the loving connection between us. God's unconditional acceptance and love for me and His perfect care have become my resting place of total security.

It's amazing to see how God works as we strive toward a new way of being, where we let Him lead.

In the spring of 2016, I had opportunities to see God provide dramatic reassurance for this new way of being.

As I was writing the proposal for this book, an opportunity came up for me to train consultants in one of the most prestigious consulting firms in the world. I had inquired with them about potential training work two years prior, but nothing had come of it. Then, out of the blue, they contacted me.

Back when I reached out to the firm, this opportunity would have been a dream come true. I would have jumped at the chance for a training contract. But at the end of 2015, God told me that in 2016 I was supposed to focus on writing the proposal for this book and not do traditional time management training. God had confirmed this to me through prayer and through a passage of Scripture. His words to me in this regard had given me enormous peace. I felt that He wanted me to turn down the firm's contract despite the fact that in the worldly sense it was an incredible opportunity, including the financial benefit of working with a top-tier global client.

Deciding not to work with the firm was hard, but I did so in faith that being under the Lord's guiding, protective hand was more important than anything else. And God took care of me. In the four weeks prior to turning down that contract, I had one new coaching client sign up. In the week after, four new clients signed up with me. All of this new business brought in over double the revenue I would have received from doing the training. And it still left me with time to move forward with writing the proposal for this book that God put on my heart.

God didn't have to reward my obedience in that way. I would do it all again regardless of the financial results. But it was so neat to see that obedience clearly led to abundance in this situation!

A few weeks later, I took a Monday afternoon off of work to attend a Bethel Breakout session for worship leaders. I could have just gone to the evening concert, and that's what made sense from a "practical" point of view. But when I prayed about it, I really felt like God wanted me to be there for the afternoon discussion too. So a fellow worship leader from my church and I attended together and got to hear wisdom from the singers who were performing at the worship concert that night and listen to a great message about doing everything in our lives from identity instead of for identity.

All in all, I allowed myself about nine precious hours on that Monday to make worship and engaging my connection with the Lord my priority. I knew I still had a great deal to do back at the office. But I felt a deep sense of peace and joy that I was in exactly the right place in the moment. I trusted God with my time.

The next morning, a glitch in my website was discovered that revealed dozens of applications for my Divine Time Management group coaching program had been getting stuck in my website for over a month. Basically the applications had been saved. Praise God! But only a small number of the notifications for those applications had come to me and my assistant. Once that discovery was made, I was able to reach out to each person individually, apologize for the lack of response, and welcome them to have a conversation with me about this special Christian group coaching program.

I felt incredibly grateful that the applications were not lost, the issue was discovered, and God could use a situation where the devil tried to undermine my work for great good.

I hadn't done anything special from a strategic business point of view to uncover this technical issue. But I believe my obedience to worship the Lord opened the door for Him to work through me. Seeking what God wanted first is what illuminated the problem that had kept me from engaging with many people about how God can transform their lives through divine time management. Darkness was brought to light.

My desire is to encourage this kind of transformative power

in your life. When we trust Him and do what He says with our time, He comes through magnificently.

■ ■ ■

THE TRUST CYCLE (GOD'S WORD STYLE)

Trust is defined as a "firm belief in the reliability, truth, or ability of someone or something."[5]

The word is used over 150 times in the Bible. In fact, one of the huge themes in the Word is the importance of trust in the Lord. When trust is placed in Him, God's people prosper—when they don't, they flounder.

If you employ no other advice from this book other than trusting in God more than your own abilities to manage your time, you have made an enormous stride toward receiving God's best.

So how do you go about strengthening trust with God? In relationship psychology, there's something known as the trust cycle.[6] It is used to explain how

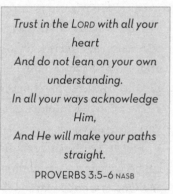

Trust in the Lord with all your heart
And do not lean on your own understanding.
In all your ways acknowledge Him,
And He will make your paths straight.
PROVERBS 3:5-6 NASB

trust is built or eroded. In the trust cycle, a need is communicated to someone who you hope will be able to meet that need. Then the need is either met or not met. Based on your perception

---

[5] *Oxford Living Dictionaries,* s.v. "trust," accessed January 18, 2017, https://en.oxforddictionaries.com/definition/trust.

[6] Danny Silk, *Keep Your Love On! Connection, Communication & Boundaries* (Redding, CA: Loving on Purpose, 2013), 96.

of whether the person's response satisfies or does not satisfy your need, then trust is either built or eroded.

> *Do not be anxious about anything, but in every situation, by prayer and petition, with thanksgiving, present your requests to God. And the peace of God, which transcends all understanding, will guard your hearts and your minds in Christ Jesus.*
>
> PHILIPPIANS 4:6-7

In some respects, you can use this definition of trust to understand how to strengthen trust with God. The most important thing you can draw from this understanding is that God wants you to express your needs to Him. God knows what your needs are but He desires you to consciously choose to come to Him and entrust your needs to His care.

However, the relational psychology definition of trust is still an incomplete picture of the kind of trust that God calls you and me to have in Him. In our text-message age, it's easy to get the attitude, "Well I prayed to God about it and didn't get a response in five minutes or less, so He must not hear or care and can't be trusted."

But the truth is, to experience God's best you've got to have a much deeper understanding of trust in God. This means trusting God is who He says He is, God can do what He says He can do, and God loves and cares for you even when you can't see or feel it yet. I find trust in God strengthens when you recall your personal experiences—the times when God came through for you, and the testimonies of others, which can be so encouraging. (When I'm struggling, I think about the amazing ways God has come through for me.) And most important, you need to build trust in the reliability of God based on what is in the Bible.

The Bible tells us:

But do not forget this one thing, dear friends: With
the Lord a day is like a thousand years, and a thousand
years are like a day. The Lord is not slow in keeping
His promise, as some understand slowness. Instead He
is patient with you, not wanting anyone to perish, but
everyone to come to repentance.

(2 Peter 3:8–9)

God's Word also reveals that the trust He desires of us is one
built on a deep faith in His character and faithfulness:

And without faith it is impossible to please God, because
anyone who comes to Him must believe that He exists
and that He rewards those who earnestly seek Him.

(Hebrews 11:6)

Through the stories of the Bible, you see that God is trust-
worthy but He is not necessarily Speedy Gonzales! Abraham
waited twenty-five years—until he was one hundred—for the
fulfillment of the promise of his son Isaac's birth; King David
endured fifteen years of hardship between when he was anointed
king and when he became king, and there are so many other
examples of God's faithfulness and unique timing in the fulfillment of His promises.

Even with total trust in Him, things won't necessarily happen as we think they should. But God is still faithful—and even
so honest as to let you know that some amazing people of faith
have not, and will not, receive the fulfillment of their promises
this side of heaven (see Hebrews 11:39). We have to trust God
with a perspective that spans longer-term than the bounds of
our time on earth.

The trust cycle, as presented in God's Word, is that you first express your needs. Then, regardless of whether God answers according to your hopes and desired timing, you choose to have faith that He hears you (see 1 John 5:14), that He cares about your needs (see 1 Pet. 5:7), that He can meet those needs (see Phil. 4:19), and that He will work everything for good in His perfect way (see Rom. 8:28).

I fully believe that God wants to show you how deeply He cares for you and that He can be completely trusted. I pray that as you do the trust-strengthening exercises in the remainder of this chapter, God will quickly and swiftly show you His power and ability to come through for you. If you're really struggling, simply say, "God, show me how much you love me today" or "God, show me how you are my protector and provider today." And He will answer you in personally meaningful ways.

Then, even if He doesn't act quickly or in the way that you expect on some big prayer requests, choose to trust. God is sovereign. More than you or I do, He knows what is His best for us, both now and into all eternity.

> "For my thoughts are not your thoughts,
>   neither are your ways my ways,"
>   declares the LORD.
> "As the heavens are higher than the earth,
>   so are my ways higher than your ways
>   and my thoughts than your thoughts."
>
> (Isaiah 55:8–9)

So now, grab your water bottle and get ready for some trust-strengthening exercises!

Trust-Strengthening Exercise: Decluttering Your Schedule

Before I began my first draft of this exercise, I went to God to ask Him what He wanted written about how we can strengthen our trust in Him by decluttering our schedules. One of the ways that I experience prayer is through conversation with God where we go back and forth with each other just like I would with another person. I know some people are familiar with this kind of prayer and others aren't. That's OK. You don't need to communicate with God in this way, but I think it's good to know it's possible. I just loved our dialogue so much that I decided to put it right in this book.

It went something like this:

Hi, God! In chapter 2 I'm going to talk to readers about decluttering their schedules. You have inspired me to write this book. I want to share what You want people to know on this subject. I'm so excited to help others experience a new way of defining their priorities.

Elizabeth, people really need to do about half of what they do.

Really?

Yes, really. People think that because they can do, they should do. American culture especially has this tendency. People feel guilty for just being normal and taking time to rest or be present in the moment. I want My children to count on Me, and to still themselves to experience the comfort of My presence.

You're right. I find myself falling into that trap sometimes.

People stay so busy doing this and that, and not really taking the time to be with Me. Even during worship, they often think about where they're going to brunch or who they should say hi to after the service. That saddens Me. There is much more in store for them.

God, I'm so sorry that hurts Your heart. We don't mean to neglect our relationship with You, but I can see how it happens. So how do You want us to decide what we do or don't do?

I want My people to stop living out of their minds and start living out of their hearts. If they find themselves consistently dreading something or doing it solely as a duty, they shouldn't be doing it. I want my children to be diligent in the things that they are committed to do, such as serving their bosses well and loving their families. But beyond that, I want them to do what I lead them to do, which will primarily be based on desire; it shouldn't feel like a heavy burden.

So we still need to do things like go to work, pay taxes, and drive our kids to school, even if it's not what we want to do all the time. But we shouldn't take on optional activities that we dread. That even means letting go of some things that aren't life giving even if they might naturally seem holy, like volunteering for a certain organization or going to a particular Bible study. Right?

Correct. There are times I'll ask people to do things they don't feel like doing out of obedience, and I'll make that very clear to them. But for My people who are delighting in Me, I give

them the desires of their heart, so I want them to live out of
those desires (Psalm 37:4). I want them to have more time
and space to just be *with Me.*

In light of what we know about God's desires for us, I would like you to go through this practical decluttering exercise. It will feel great to clear up some time to reconnect with God or to get closer to Him.

- **STEP ONE:** Lay out everything in your schedule on a table. You could print out your calendar, write each activity on a separate sheet of paper, draw a chart, or really approach this however you want. The point is that I want you to have a clear visual representation of all of the different commitments filling your schedule.

- **STEP TWO:** Separate out the must-do activities, such as work, and the optional ones. Pray about the must-do activities, asking God if you're spending the right amount of time on each one. Then wait for His answer on whether you should do more, less, or stay the same. Many of these activities may remain status quos, but pay attention if you feel a tug on your heart, an idea in your mind, or even a vision of how some activities should take up more or less time in your life.

- **STEP THREE:** Once you sense God's guidance regarding potentially devoting more or less time to your must-do activities, ask God how and when the changes should happen. Write down what you think He is speaking into your heart in response to your inquiry to Him. Continue to pray about it, and when you sense God's clear direction, act on it. You could add these prayer requests to your to-do list, or put reminders in your calendar about them. Sometimes the answer will be "wait" or "pray." In those instances, try to remind yourself to trust that God can and will reveal what to do—or not do—at just the right time. You don't need to force a change to happen prematurely.

■ **STEP FOUR:** As you await clarity regarding your must-do activities, focus your attention on those that are optional, one by one. Consider each, paying attention to the feelings that emerge. Do you feel excitement? Dread? Fear? Light? Sober? Giddy? Let your feelings guide this exercise. Try not to think too hard about it. Do not write a list of pros and cons. Do not focus on the expectations of others. Pay attention to your energy level and spontaneous emotional response to each activity from within.

■ **STEP FIVE:** If you feel a heavy emotion regarding any of the activities, ask yourself: *Why is that?* Then ask God whether the activity should be done less often or eliminated from your schedule. Pay attention to what He says and let go of preconceived notions about what you should or shouldn't want to do.

■ **STEP SIX:** When you feel light, positive emotions regarding any of the activities, ask yourself: *Why am I responding this way?* Then ask God if you should increase, or maintain, the amount of time you spend in that area. Stay attuned to His presence through prayer for guidance.

■ **STEP SEVEN:** Regularly journal your thoughts. I believe you will find that God will tell you to reduce or eliminate tasks that give you a sense of dread or heaviness and to increase those that bring you joy. But God does not fit into a box, and there may be times where you actually sense the opposite. Keep making time with God a priority. As you seek Him, He will reveal the right answers.

■ **STEP EIGHT:** Start to take action on what you feel is right. Some changes may be easy, things that you can do right away. For others it may take longer to really figure out what you should do and when. You don't need to push this; there is no set timeline, unless God makes one clear. For example, sometimes I've sensed God telling me that I need to stop something immediately. Other times, God has directed me to wait until a certain time, such as the end of the year, before making a change. Sometimes God even tells me that there is a pending change but gives me no specific direction on when or how that will happen. Actively engage with whatever information God gives you, and let go of guilt about cutting back on activities in your schedule without putting anything tangible back in. "Because God told me so," is a good enough reason to do or not do anything. No further explanation needed.

Through this process, you will declutter your schedule so that you start to have more and more free space personally and professionally. In our overscheduled culture, that may feel a little bit awkward at first. It requires trust that everyone and everything will be OK without you always being involved. It requires trust that you won't miss out. But decluttering your schedule plays an essential role in freeing up time you can spend ministering to God's heart by investing in your relationship with Him. In lessening your activity, you learn to trust God more, and you can discover more of God's best.

■ ■ ■

Trust-Strengthening Exercise: Investing in Your Relationship with God

God's an easy date.

If He were filling out an online dating profile, under "Favorite Places" He would put something like, *I'm happy to be anywhere, as long as I'm with the people I love*, and actually mean it.

God is head over heels for you; 1 John 4:10 tells us, "This is love: not that we loved God, but that he loved us and sent his Son as an atoning sacrifice for our sins." Consider the magnitude of that love. The Father God really, really, really loves Jesus, His only begotten Son. But in His amazing love for us, He allowed the one person who ever walked in perfect communion with Him, and who loved Him perfectly, to suffer and die so that we could all know and love Him. That was the highest cost He could have possibly paid in His love for us. And He paid it.

God wants a relationship with you. Once you're in Christ, that's possible (see Eph. 2:18). You have an unlimited-access VIP pass to communicate with God anywhere, anytime.

But to take advantage of that access, and to receive God's best in your relationship with Him and all areas of your life, you'll need to trust God enough to really invest in the relationship instead of keeping Him at a distance. Here are some key areas where you may need to increase your trust and some trust-building exercises to help you move forward.

* * *

Trust that God Wants to Be with You: It feels cliché to say this, but it's true so it must be said. Much of how you initially view God has to do with your experience of your earthly father. If your dad was kind and loving and delighted in you, then you were probably inclined to think that God is kind and loving and delighted in you. If your dad was absent physically or emotionally, you may have developed thoughts of God as absent physically or emotionally. To come into a deeper relationship with God, you need to stop projecting your experience of fathers onto God and start looking at who God says He is through His Word. The Bible tells you that God delights in and rejoices over you (see Isa. 62:4–5 and Zeph. 3:17). God's never disinterested in you. He's always thinking about how He can bless you, love you, protect you, and provide for you. He is always interested in being part of every detail of your life, and there is nothing that He wouldn't do for you. God thinks of you with joy even when you ignore Him and disobey Him, because He loves you no matter what. God always has and always will delight in you, want the best for you, and want to be close to you.

TRUST-BUILDING STEP: Even if you've never experienced an earthly father figure genuinely wanting to be with you, you need to take God at His word by faith that His face lights up at the thought of you. Then ask God to show you in clear ways how much He wants to be with you—no matter what. When you do, He will come through.

Trust that God Won't Hurt You: Depending on your experience with your earthly father, or authority figures in general, and based on any teaching you've already received about God's nature, you may have a little—or a lot—of trepidation. What will God do or say if you approach Him? Will He judge or punish you? Will He tell you to do something that you don't want to do? It is true that God is a God of justice. In the Old Testament, God was gracious and merciful with people's sins. (If He wasn't, the human race would have ended with Adam and Eve.) But there were also times when God's wrath swiftly wiped out thousands of people as a punishment for their sins.

In the New Testament, we see a God whom we can approach without fear because He chose to put the punishment of our sins on Jesus once and for all instead of making us pay that price.

> We are made right with God by placing our faith in Jesus Christ. And this is true for everyone who believes, no matter who we are. For everyone has sinned; we all fall short of God's glorious standard. Yet God, in his grace, freely makes us right in his sight. He did this through Christ Jesus when he freed us from the penalty for our sins. For God presented Jesus as the sacrifice for sin. People are made right with God when they believe that Jesus sacrificed his life, shedding his blood. This sacrifice shows that God was being fair when he held back and did not punish those who sinned in times past, for he was looking ahead and including them in what he would do in this present time. God did this to demonstrate his righteousness, for he himself is fair and just, and he makes sinners right in his sight when they believe in Jesus.
>
> (Romans 3:22–26 NLT)

Today, God is still a God of justice, but because Jesus covered our sins, you and I are currently in a time of divine grace. We can now approach God directly—instead of through priests like in the Old Testament—and with confidence that we're His beloved children (see Rom. 8:15). God does say that He disciplines those He loves, like any good father would (see Heb. 12:5–11). But He will never forsake you, maliciously hurt or harm you, and He gives you good and perfect gifts (see James 1:17).

That means that whatever God tells you to do or not do, or chooses to give or not give you, is for your good. There have been times I've been so angry and frustrated at God for not giving me what I wanted when I wanted it. But again and again, I learn that God was protecting me by using every circumstance to bring me to His best.

TRUST-BUILDING STEP: Take time to communicate with God. That could start out as simple as telling Him what's on your mind while you lie in bed at night, writing to Him in a journal, going to a church service, or listening to worship music. Once you get comfortable talking to God (and realize He doesn't bite), ask Him to speak to you and see what He says. You can expect that, as you're beginning to build your relationship with the Lord, His voice will be gentle and kind toward you. He loves and accepts you right now, right where you are at.

Once you have trust that God wants to spend time with you and desires to help—not hurt you—then you're ready to free up the time and mental space to make that connection possible. That requires turning off the external and internal noises that distract so you can focus on God with all your heart.

Trust that You Can Turn Off the External Noise: Especially with the ever-increasing presence of technology in our lives, it's possible to never have silence. You can still connect with God when there is some external activity. For example, when I'm in worship services I often grab my journal to scribble down what God is speaking to me. But when we're listening to TV, radio, people, or music that distracts us from God instead of drawing us toward Him, it's hard to really fully connect with God. That's why I think it's essential to not have external noise for at least an hour a day. That could mean not talking on the phone on your commute or when you cook dinner. That could be getting up earlier than the other people in your house to have personal quiet time. That could happen by going on a walk and silencing your phone. Exactly what it is doesn't matter as much as that you give yourself time, whenever possible, to hear God's voice. That will be possible when you're not listening to something else instead.

TRUST-BUILDING STEP: Find sixty minutes every day to devote to being with God. This may not be easy, but you can break it up into multiple parts such as two thirty-minute segments. You can also do this while taking a walk, driving in the car, doing household chores, or getting ready in the morning. You don't need to sit down with a Bible and journal to make this happen. But you do need to have your mind intentionally focused on God. I am positive that this should be at the top of your priority list. There is no better use of your time. You can only enter into God's best if you commit to quality time with Him.

Trust that You Can Turn Off the Internal Noise: One of the biggest struggles I've faced in trying to become more intimate with God is turning off the internal noise in my head. When I get excited about something, focused, afraid, or experience any strong emotion or desire, my mental neurons start firing a million miles a minute. I can be sitting at my dining room table with my Bible in front of me, but I struggle to read it because my mind is on how to reply to a difficult e-mail, how to coordinate an upcoming trip, or any number of challenges. Sometimes, I'll go through seasons where I wake up at about four thirty in the morning with my mind churning on a particular topic. (That's annoying.) I don't have the perfect answer for how to turn off the internal noise. It's something that I need to address anew whenever it comes up. But I have found that the first and most important step to achieving internal quiet is to think about God's sovereignty and His power. Or, put God back in His place and put yourself back in yours.

TRUST-BUILDING STEP: When I put God back in His place by praying, reading His Word, and listening to worship music, I then can put myself back in mine: a child who is perfectly cared for by her perfect heavenly Father. Nothing is impossible for God. That's a secure place of trust. I don't need to exhaust myself over how to work everything out, because God is actively at work on my behalf to take care of everything in the best way possible. The next time you're distracted by internal noise, turn your eyes to God and allow your challenges to fade away in His presence. As I heard a wise person once say, "Worry is a temporary bout of atheism."

When you have those times when you continue to struggle to get out of your mind, you may want to try this wonderful tip that I picked up from one of my Divine Time Management coaching clients. It is to focus on being very present to your body and to your senses. For example, stop and ask yourself what you see and consciously look at the environment around you. As you do, pause to think about what you hear, smell, and so on. Getting in tune with what's happening outside our own heads can put us in a position to get more in tune with God.

Investing time and effort in your relationship with God is a huge part of trusting Him—trusting that He wants to be with you, that He won't hurt you, and that you can disengage from distractions to find a place of peace in His perfect care. When you're in that kind of relationship with God, you'll be open to receive blessings without striving.

TRUST STORY FROM JOHN

Me: *One of the big things that I've been learning through Divine Time Management is that it's less about focusing on ourselves— what we can do or not do, figure out or not figure out—and more about turning to God and putting trust in Him at the center.*

John: *That is exactly what I've been experiencing. This week, I haven't really done much in terms of the new habits I want to build, and things have actually been quite busy. But I've been asking God to show me that He can work things out so that I can rest and take care of myself, and I don't have to push myself so hard all the time or become the "super-organizer" to maximize my time (although I do think I could improve my routines).*

A perfect example was yesterday—out of the blue, my boss instant messaged me and then we talked on the phone. He had decided certain things needed to happen. What I expected would be a long process (and require a lot of effort on my part)

> suddenly got "settled" with him clearly laying out my next steps
> in a way that was exactly what I would have desired. He wrote
> a great follow-up email this morning that sealed what will be
> expected of me in my new role. So I didn't need to work/worry/
> stress about it; God moved.
>
> This whole week has been like that—connecting with people
> at the right time ("Oh, so the reason I went to my desk when
> I wasn't planning on it was that my colleague really needed
> some encouragement."), relationships going smoothly, inspired
> thoughts. It's definitely the hand of God working. He is so good!

■   ■   ■

Trust-Strengthening Exercise: Building Enough Faith to Rest in Him

In the Old Testament, if you did work on the Sabbath, it could
lead to the death penalty (see Exod. 35:1–3, Num. 15:32–36).
And the religious people of the day made a whole lot of rules
around what constituted work on the Sabbath, covering everything from cooking to taking care of animals, and anything in
between.

When Jesus arrived on the scene, He stood against a lot of
the legalism around keeping the Sabbath (see Matt. 12:1–13). But
that doesn't mean that the Sabbath no longer holds importance.

God's people taking time to rest is something He takes
seriously—super seriously. Keeping the Sabbath is one of the ten
commandments, right up there with not murdering or committing adultery. So a huge part of trusting God with your time
means refraining from work for one twenty-four-hour period

each week, so that you can focus on your relationship with God and with the people He has put in your life.

I know that different Christian denominations have different views of exactly when a Sabbath rest should happen, so please follow what God has put on your heart to be right for you. It's important that you have a clean conscience before God. In my case, what this looks like is that from late Saturday afternoon to late Sunday afternoon, I try not to do any work. My church has Saturday night services, in addition to Sunday morning ones, so I often go to church on Saturday night to kick off my Sabbath. For me, that means avoiding business activities and those tasks that feel like chores, such as housecleaning or errands I don't enjoy. Then I'm free on Sunday evening to wrap up any of those items since I started my Sabbath on Saturday.

I most prefer investing my Sabbath time in going to church, having extra-long quiet times with God, spending time in nature, and visiting with friends and family. The Sabbath period gives me much-needed mental space to remember that there's a God—and I'm not Him. It helps me to trust Him that everything will get done that needs to get done without me constantly being productive.

I believe that your weekly Sabbath rest and daily moments with God, where you pause from your activity to acknowledge Him, are the greatest possible enhancements to your productivity and the fastest route to receiving all of the blessings God wants you to enjoy in your life. Not only are there practical implications in terms of the stress reduction benefits of a break[7] but also a lot of God's blessings come in "if, then" format.

---

[7] Joe Robinson, "The Secret to Increased Productivity: Taking Time Off," *Entrepreneur*, October 2014, accessed January 18, 2017, https://www.entrepreneur.com/article/237446.

"If you keep your feet from breaking the Sabbath
and from doing as you please on my holy day,
if you call the Sabbath a delight
and the LORD's holy day honorable,
and if you honor it by not going your own way
and not doing as you please or speaking idle words,
then you will find your joy in the LORD,
and I will cause you to ride in triumph on the heights of
the land
and to feast on the inheritance of your father Jacob."
For the mouth of the LORD has spoken.

(Isaiah 58:13–14)

Basically, God lays out some really good blessings that arise from keeping the Sabbath. And, yes, not honoring the Sabbath causes negative implications in our lives. So it's best to keep it. If you take time off each week as an act of trusting God with your time, you not only benefit from rest, but you also open yourself to receive a whole bunch of extra blessings God can pour out. If you don't keep the Sabbath, you not only miss out on the downtime but also He can't give you as many good things. So trust in God enough to take a Sabbath. It is essential to receiving His best.

TRUST-BUILDING STEP: If you haven't already developed a Sabbath habit, I encourage you to start one. Consider the best ways you could honor God on Sunday or another day during the week and try it out. In doing this, you will give yourself a weekly opportunity to radically trust the Lord with your time and experience the highest quality of relationship with Him and the highest quality of life He desires to give you.

* * *

As a word of caution: If your natural tendency leans toward worrying about perfectly following God's commands by your own strength, recognizing the Sabbath can throw you into a tizzy of striving to fit everything into six days a week. This makes the Sabbath feel like a burden. I know that's what happened for me when I first made attempts to follow this commandment more fully.

It's true; it's easier to take a day off when you think ahead about what needs to be done and take care of it in advance. That's good stewardship of your time. However, we're not supposed to turn the Sabbath rest into something we can "earn" through working super hard throughout the week. If you do, you've missed the point. The Sabbath is a gift and an opportunity to trust that God will provide for all of your needs regardless of whether or not you've used your time perfectly during the previous six days—and even if you wonder how everything will get done if you take a day off. When I've trusted God enough to take a Sabbath rest even when I didn't feel like I could logically afford to not work, things worked out for God's best. I've seen meetings get canceled, deadlines extend, and time open up in all sorts of other ways. God will come through for you when you put Him first.

Make taking the Sabbath about trust in God, not trust in self.

■ ■ ■

Trust-Strengthening Exercise: Loving People So Much You Let Go

Another critical area of trust in God with our time is in how we relate to other people's needs. It often seems like people prioritize action in one of two ways: they respond to any expressed or perceived human need, or they focus on what they believe is the most important external task at hand, without wavering when a people situation arises. For example, you may have one coworker who will drop everything she is doing to help when she overhears a conversation about someone having an issue. Then you may have another colleague who will only assist with something when you ask her directly. And she will get to it only once it becomes the highest priority from among her other tasks.

Depending on where you fall in this spectrum, trusting God with your time looks different. For those of us who hop in and try to fix everything—even when we're not asked—complete trust in God will mean choosing not to get involved unless we're certain that's what God has said to do. You will have to let go of the wrong belief that it's always best for you to help. When God asks you to support someone or do something, it will lead to His best. But if God is not calling you to help someone or do something, you could actually hinder yourself or the other person. Perhaps your help keeps them from leaning on God instead of you. Or, maybe you are acting on a need to feel in control. Most who try to help mean well. But feeling a compulsion to always jump into a situation is fear based not trust based.

Alternatively, if you're a person who sticks to your task list no matter what, for you to develop trust in God you'll have to loosen control of your schedule and allow God to change it when He wants to. That doesn't mean you need to immediately respond in every situation. But when God tells you to take an unplanned phone call, spontaneously visit a friend, or take care of a family member—your test is to trust God enough to take time for the unexpected.

TRUST-BUILDING STEP: Spend some time with God evaluating the relationships in your life, both personally and professionally. Then ask the Lord if you're doing what you're doing out of a place of trust or out of a place of fear. If you think that your actions may be fear driven, ask God to show you how to choose a different response to people in upcoming situations.

TRUST IS ENOUGH

At the core, trust in God really is enough. God says that when we trust Him, He will direct us and come through for us. That includes blessing us with the time and every other good thing that we need to receive God's best in our lives.

Once you've begun to trust God through the trust-strengthening exercises in this chapter, you'll begin to understand the truth of who you really are in light of who He really is. In the next section of this book, we'll explore what it means to love and live out of your true identity.

Reflection Exercise: **ENOUGH TIME**

I would like you to ask yourself this simple, critical question: *What would it look like to trust God with my time?*

I've noticed that I stress about time when I start to think that there won't be enough time or everything won't get done. When I recognize I'm operating out of fear, I can then make a choice. I can choose to trust God: He is in control, and when I'm obedient to what He wants me to do, moment by moment, everything will be OK.

Trusting God helps me enjoy life more, and less stress creates room for God to work within me. I've found that when I let go, He works in amazing ways to get things done, provide help for me, or make me realize the things that I thought were so important actually aren't worth fretting over. Plus, as anyone would be, I'm a much lovelier person when I trust God, instead of being super uptight.

Let's make a commitment to focus on trust in God, not ourselves, with our time.

God's best,
Elizabeth

> *"But blessed is the one who trusts in the LORD,*
> *whose confidence is in him.*
> *They will be like a tree planted by the water*
> *that sends out its roots by the stream.*
> *It does not fear when heat comes;*
> *its leaves are always green.*
> *It has no worries in a year of drought*
> *and never fails to bear fruit."*

JEREMIAH 17:7–8

. . .

LOVE FOR YOUR TRUE IDENTITY

CHAPTER 3

Images We Create to Earn Love

*"Self-help is no help at all. Self-sacrifice is the way, my way,
to finding yourself, your true self. What kind of deal is it to get
everything you want but lose yourself? What could you ever
trade your soul for?"*

MATTHEW 16:24–26 MSG

The year 2015 was a time of great breakthrough in relationships...for my friends. Every woman who was in her thirties in my local Christian group, except me, got married. I broke up with my boyfriend in February of that year and was single the rest of the year.

In retrospect, I see how that was God's amazing protection of me, as He was doing the deep work of securing my identity in Him. But at the time, it felt excruciatingly difficult. It's one thing to be single when you want to be in a relationship. It's another to feel left behind.

When one of my friends got married at the end of that year, I was so happy to celebrate her relationship with a wonderful man who loved God and loved her. I had kept hoping that God might have someone wonderful for me too...I waited until the last possible day to send in the RSVP card just in case I might have a guest to bring.

On the day I sent the RSVP card confirming that it would be "just me," I cried.

To help psych myself up for the big day, I planned a fantastic outfit that I couldn't have worn in my day-to-day life. It included a cashmere sweater with fox fur that encircled my shoulders and a new birdcage hat. I have quite an extensive hat collection that I wear often. But the opportunity to wear a fabulous new hat is always a joyful event.

I prayed that God would take my eyes and heart off myself and instead focus them on the incredible joy of my dear friend's beautiful day. I felt selfish for even making any of this about me when it wasn't; it was about her marriage.

The wedding was a gorgeous time of worshipping the Lord and celebrating the couple's love. Mission accomplished. Happy face on and heart on God.

But the reception presented more of a struggle for me. I rode the elevator up to the second-floor ballroom with two others; one was a friend I hadn't seen in a while. He said, "Hi, Elizabeth! Great to see you. This is my fiancée. Have you met her before?"

Deep breaths. Remember, Elizabeth, happy, happy, joy, joy. God, please help me to be happy for others and to remember their blessing isn't a judgment on me and my seeming lack of blessing in this area.

I put on my best smile. "Yes, I think we've met before. Congratulations!"

After stepping out of the elevator, I happily milled about and received quite a few compliments on my new hat.

Then I headed to my table, where I knew a friend would also be seated. She had been single for as long as I had known her—about six years—so I looked forward to the opportunity to commiserate on our singleness.

Not quite what happened...

Soon after we started talking, she understandably informed me of her happy news. She had not only started dating someone but was married! No joke.

Many times before and many times since, I've been able to simply be delighted when my amazing friends are blessed with amazing husbands. But on that particular night, delight was not the *d* word that surfaced. Instead, despair and discouragement were my companions. It was a beautiful night, and I know I was a beautiful addition to the night, but my heart was heavy.

I made my exit early. As soon as I got to my car, I started crying.

But then God started hugging me as the tears rolled down. And God's hugs are very comforting...

He spoke to my heart, letting me know it was OK to be sad. He wanted me to be honest, open, and authentic with Him— and He prefers a hot mess of authentic tears any day over a perfect "plastic princess."

What's so ironic is that this plastic princess was who I'd often thought I needed to be to make God happy. A beautiful, godly woman who does what's right, feels what's right, and is always hopeful and positive even when she's single and doesn't want to be.

Through this situation and others, God has shown that we should bust out of the papier-mâché identities we assume in a futile attempt to earn love, and embrace our true selves.

God knew what He was doing when He created you and me. Any fake stuff we put on is a cheap imitation of what He intended and a waste of precious time. To truly experience each moment of the joyful life God intends for us, we need to be authentic.

*   *   *

WHY IDENTITY IS CRITICAL

Identity is so critical because by nature we want to align with who we believe we are. Our identity, our sense of what makes us "us," has implications on what we do, what we say, what we wear, how we spend our time, where we feel we belong, where our money goes, and our belief in what is possible.

That's why when I start working with coaching clients, I ask them to stop saying things like, "I'm a procrastinator," or "I'm a people-pleaser." Because if they're constantly saying these phrases, they are claiming the wrong identity. Actions that they want to change become just part of who they are. It becomes almost impossible for them to change because it's literally a form of self-cursing. If you want to step into God's best for your life with divine time management, you must get to know and love your true identity in Christ.

Knowing and loving your true spiritual identity is not an easy feat. Your earthly identity started to be formed even before you were born, through characteristics from your biological mother and father. This came through their physical DNA as well as how your parents thought and felt about you and themselves during your gestation period.

Then, after you were born, how you perceived yourself began through the reflection of the human mirrors around you. If your parents' eyes lit up when they saw you and they were responsive to your needs, then your sense of identity was "I am a joy" and "I am worthy of care." If you experienced neglect or abuse, or other bad things, your sense of self formed differently. You may have internalized that "I'm not important" or even "I'm bad or dirty."

The process of creating a sense of identity based on the physical world around you is natural and normal. It's how God created you. But as a child of God, you can only understand the fullness of your true identity by knowing and believing what God says about your spiritual identity.

Also, you can only be truly free to receive all the good God wants to give you and to align your time with His will when you believe the truth of who God says you are. We'll dive into discovering your true identity in a much deeper sense in chapter 5. But as a little preview, here's some of what God's Word says about you and me:

> But you are a chosen people, a royal priesthood, a holy
> nation, God's special possession, that you may declare the
> praises of Him who called you out of darkness into His
> wonderful light.
>
> (1 Peter 2:9)

> Yet to all who did receive him, to those who believed in
> his name, he gave the right to become children of God.
>
> (John 1:12)

> Therefore, if anyone is in Christ, the new creation has
> come: The old has gone, the new is here!
>
> (2 Corinthians 5:17)

To fully step into all the good that God has for you with your time and all other areas of your life, you need to let go of false identities so you can embody your true one. This involves dropping the surface facades that provide a temporary confidence boost but leave you insecure at the core, and allowing God to build your true identity from the depths of who you are—a strong and sure foundation.

This process is essential for living out the most radiant you. It's how you go from constantly trying to earn love to living in the reality that a constant outpouring of love is already rightfully yours each and every moment as a child of God.

In the coming sections, we'll address false identities that keep you from being the true "you" such as:

- Molds you try to fit into, like "good mother" or "high achiever"
- Labels you wear, such as "smart" or "responsible" or "lazy"
- Positions you point to as validation of worth
- Possessions you cling to for security
- Generational patterns you think you need to follow

I encourage you to allow God to reveal to you where it's time to let go so that you can begin living out of your true identity, acting out of your true identity, and in turn receive all of the blessings God has for you as He brings you into His best.

Although these identities may feel "safe," in reality, they keep you trapped below the line of your privilege. It's time to bust out.

False Identity: Molds You Try to Fit

Some kids are natural rebels. They try to go against the grain however and whenever they can. I was the opposite. At a young age, I learned to squeeze myself into a mold in my desire for love, attention, and approval.

It started with trying to figure out what it meant to be a "good daughter" and "good friend." Then it transitioned to trying to understand how to be an honors student, a scholarship winner, a top job candidate, and a successful young entrepreneur.

To be clear: none of these are bad things. It's good to be a blessing to your family, to do well in life, etc. But the issue is that in this process I wasn't focused on being authentically myself. Instead, I strived to achieve some external standard of perfection—or at least to get a solid A. So I decided what I would wear, which activities I did, how I spoke, and how I showed up in the world based on these external standards.

Since I'm so good at fitting into molds, I consistently got positive feedback for my performance. But I ended up feeling tired and a little lost and lonely. Having to constantly put on a show is a lot of work and keeps you from relaxing and having moments of genuine connection where you're seen, known, and appreciated just for being you.

My guess is that I'm not alone.

It seems to me that in Christian circles especially, people can feel a lot of pressure to be a certain way, act a certain way, and most important, to have everything appear a certain way. But Romans 12:2 tells us, "Do not conform to the pattern of this world, but be transformed by the renewing of your mind. Then you will be able to test and approve what God's will is—his good, pleasing and perfect will."

I would like you to take a moment now to reflect on where you might be trying to fit a "mold." For instance, consider whether you are more concerned about conforming to external standards of perfection than about authentically living out these areas of your life:

- **Core identity:** What it means to be human, to be a man or woman
- **Spiritual identity:** What it means to be a Christian, a Christ follower, a son or daughter of God
- **Family identity:** What it means to be a son, daughter, husband, wife, dad, mom, cousin, uncle, grandparent, or other member of a family
- **Other personal relationships:** What it means to be a friend, church member, PTA member, neighbor, etc.
- **Cultural and ethnic identity:** What it means to be American, Irish, blue collar, educated, etc.
- **Professional identity:** What it means to be a good employee, business owner, manager, professor, teacher, etc.

If you're struggling to tell if you're being authentic or smashing yourself into a mold, here are a few signs to look for:

You're trying to hide something. For example, I have sometimes felt insecure about the fact that I don't do a lot of cooking. Because I envisioned that as part of the mold of a "good wife" or a "good mother," I thought it was bad for men to know that cooking wasn't my greatest interest or strength. Now that I know the mold is a false ideal I was trying to achieve, I'm a lot more bold. I've even gone so far as to let men know on the first date that I'm not much of a chef. I now recognize that I can be a great wife and mother without having amazing culinary skills, so I have nothing to hide.

Another sign you may be trying to fit a mold and living a false identity is that you find yourself doing many things because you feel like you "should" do them, things you really don't want to do. For example, you volunteer to sew costumes for the school play when you really dislike sewing, because you think that's what "good moms" do. Or, you check work e-mail over the weekend when nothing is truly urgent, because that's what "committed employees" do, and you find it draining. Or perhaps you accept a friend's invitation to get together when you really want to decline, because that's what "good friends" do.

I'm not saying to never make a choice to do something despite not feeling like it—sacrificial love, especially as a spouse or parent, is necessary and deeply satisfying. There are absolutely times when I make a choice to put my wants or needs aside to do things for a friend or family member, like changing travel plans to be present at an important event, or staying up talking when I'm really exhausted because someone is in a rough spot. But I don't think you should find yourself perpetually giving beyond what you can with a spirit of generosity simply because you feel like you have to, in order to fit a mold of "good" anything.

When you give more time and energy than God tells you to on even really good activities—you're out of alignment with God. When you're out of alignment with God's will, you'll not be able to achieve the state of being God intends for you. Instead of peace and joy, you'll end up in burnout and fatigue. And you'll miss out on whatever God did want you to do with your time instead.

However, once you identify and break free of these molds, you'll be able to use your time in alignment with God's plan for you.

Breaking-Free Exercise: Molds You Try to Fit

The first step to breaking free of molds is to recognize that they're present. Take some time to reflect on the different categories of molds listed and ask God to reveal to you if you're trying to fit yourself into a mold in one or more of the areas.

Think about how your effort to fit these molds causes you to do things that aren't aligned with your true identity. If you're not sure, make it a point to take note of when you find yourself wanting to hide some information about yourself or when you do something that's not truly necessary out of compulsion instead of desire. You can keep track of these instances in a note in your phone for a week.

Then ask yourself, *If I wasn't trying to fit into a mold of a "good this" or "good that," what choice would I make?*

Now you can change the behavior, even gradually. It may feel awkward at first to say no where you might have previously said yes and vice versa. But you should notice a greater level of peace, ease, flow, and alignment with God as you make choices based on your true identity.

■   ■   ■

False Identity: Labels You Wear

We generally accept that bad things people say to us or about us, such as "you're stupid" or "you can't do anything right," can have a negative impact. But God has shown me that "good" things people say that we take on as labels, or badges of honor, can be just as detrimental.

For example, it's not healthy or helpful for me to claim labels such as "planner," "responsible," or even "nice" as part of my identity. Yes, it's true that I tend to plan in advance. (It's my job for a reason.) I do tend to be responsible. And overall I am a quite pleasant person to be around.

But sometimes I don't plan as well as I should and end up

staying up late packing for a trip. I sometimes eat dessert as my meal. And there are times when I need to set a firm boundary. I'm doing what's right, but I don't come across as nice.

If I took on these "good" labels as identity, I could fall into the pride/fear trap. In this trap, I feel a smug sense of satisfaction when I live up to the label, whether it's something as small as "always on time" or as large as "top performer in the company." I could point to my congruence with that label as justification for why I'm worthy and loved. But then when I don't measure up to that label or am afraid that I might not, I start to panic and experience so much fear.

By choosing not to take on labels like "planner," I give myself freedom to act out of my true identity in the way that's most appropriate for the situation, in agreement with my capacity and desires at the moment. This freedom allows me to enter into God's best.

Also, it's simply biblical. Here's what the apostle Paul had to say about not wearing all his good labels in Philippians 3:3–9.

> For it is we who are the circumcision, we who serve God
> by his Spirit, who boast in Christ Jesus, and who put no
> confidence in the flesh—though I myself have reasons for
> such confidence.
> If someone else thinks they have reasons to put confi-
> dence in the flesh, I have more: circumcised on the eighth
> day, of the people of Israel, of the tribe of Benjamin, a
> Hebrew of Hebrews; in regard to the law, a Pharisee;
> as for zeal, persecuting the church; as for righteousness
> based on the law, faultless.
> But whatever were gains to me I now consider loss for
> the sake of Christ. What is more, I consider everything a

loss because of the surpassing worth of knowing Christ
Jesus my Lord, for whose sake I have lost all things. I
consider them garbage, that I may gain Christ and be
found in him, not having a righteousness of my own
that comes from the law, but that which is through faith
in Christ—the righteousness that comes from God on
the basis of faith.

Breaking-Free Exercise: Labels You Wear

Similar to molds, labels can be tricky and sometimes difficult
to spot. If you've been wearing them a long time, they feel comfortable and even right, like a childhood nickname.

But labels hinder your freedom to live your divine identity,
because instead of giving yourself the flexibility to authentically act like yourself in any particular situation, you're limiting
yourself to acting in a way that aligns with a "description." So
you want to expose labels and then rip off the name tag. One of
the best ways to identify labels is to observe how you talk about
yourself both out loud and in your head.

For example, I try to stop myself from saying that I'm a punctual person. Instead I might say, "I tend to be on time" or "I like
to be on time." This can be really helpful. Because if I don't base
my identity on a label, I won't be stressed if I'm a few minutes
late because "I'm a punctual person; I should always be on time."

Another way to tell when you might have taken on labels
is by paying attention to how you respond to what people say
about you. It's OK if people say nice things about you, and it's
OK to accept a compliment and even say *thank you* for it. But
avoid internalizing what people say as a standard that you need
to constantly live up to. For example, if someone thanks you for

being thoughtful, you can express your gratitude for the appreciation. But stay out of the trap of believing the lie that you need to always be whatever you think it means to be a "thoughtful person." Everything you do should be decided in your mind and heart as guided by God, not in an attempt to live up to a label.

False Identity: Positions You Point to as Validation of Worth

My senior year of college was the best of times and the worst of times for me. February of my senior year, I got hired as a staff writer for two interior design magazines. The agreement was that I would work part-time until I graduated in May and then transition into the position full-time. I was ecstatic! I had pursued this dream of working for interior design magazines since the age of fourteen. I was heading toward college graduation thinking my first job was all set. Life was pretty sweet.

Then six weeks later, I got laid off. Ouch.

Welcome to the real world, Elizabeth. Here's your severance package and a few months later, here's your college diploma. Because you were employed during the exact six weeks when all of the other positions you were interviewing for were filled, you are graduating without a job. Double ouch.

So there I was, at the end of school, during all of the final festivities, feeling pretty pitiful. I had centered my identity around my straight-A-student status and all of the awesome internships I had throughout college. Now, I found myself without a permanent position and a pretty low sense of identity and worth.

One of the end-of-school events I attended was for the Donald V. Adams Leadership Institute, which I had participated in during my time at Drake University. Don Adams himself happened to be at the reception, and in a moment of vulnerability, I expressed to him that I didn't feel like I had a lot to be proud of.

He looked at me kindly, gave me a friendly grandpa-like hug, and simply said, "I'm proud of you."

It still brings tears to my eyes to recall that moment of truth. It reminded me that my identity and worth weren't in whatever grasp I had on this or that position, academically or professionally.

I'll treasure that moment forever.

My prayer for you is that you will loosen your grasp on whatever positions you cling to as your source of identity—whether it's a certain job title, a role at church, a seat in an organization, or any other sort of "position" that you point to as your source of worth. As you loosen your grip, you'll be able to freely live in the moment, enjoying the good of your role without pride about having it or fear about losing it.

Although it may be hard for you if and when God closes a door, you'll be able to go through that change without losing your sense of self-worth. In holding loosely to everything, you'll have the agility to enter into God's best with your time and know you're good enough, no matter what position you're in or not in.

> "For whoever wants to save their life will lose it, but whoever loses their life for me will find it. What good will it be for someone to gain the whole world, yet forfeit their soul? Or what can anyone give in exchange for their soul?"
>
> (Matthew 16:25–26)

Breaking-Free Exercise: Positions You Point to as Validation of Worth

Basing our identity on titles or positions is completely acceptable in the worldly sense. Especially in the professional world, there's a huge emphasis on titles, offices, organizational charts, and so on. Position can also seem important in other parts of life, from school committees to church worship teams.

Having a position is not wrong. If God has put you in a certain place, you should accept it with humility and gratitude. But basing your identity on a position isn't OK, because positions come and positions go. You can't feel steady and secure in yourself if you build your identity on an unstable foundation.

These two questions will help you identify a problem with how you measure your worth and identity: How important is it to you that others know you have a certain position? And how willing are you to give it up? If it's highly important to you that others know and extremely difficult for you to think of giving it up, then you've got an issue. Your self-worth and identity may be wrapped up in that position.

Take a look at all the different positions you hold in your life and run them through the above two tests with honesty. If at any time you feel that your heart is not right, ask God to show you how He wants you to think about your identity apart from any position.

Finally, be willing to let anything go. Over the past few years, God has told me that I needed to step down from a number of positions, even ones I really enjoyed. It was hard to lose that sense of being known, important, and even "in control" of certain situations. But I've seen how God has used these shifts to help me base my identity more fully in Him and to open up my time for new opportunities.

To enter into God's best, no position can come ahead of the Lord.

■　■　■

False Identity: Possessions You Cling to for Security

God is really into beautiful things. With the temple, He gave instructions for elaborate gold ornamentation and tapestries. In Proverbs 31, He talks about a virtuous woman being clothed in fine linen and purple and her household being clothed in scarlet. And throughout the Old Testament, He often had the children of Israel receive tremendous plunder.

Nice things are not a problem.

Basing our identity and security on nice things, or things in general, is a problem. As one of my time management coaching clients once said, it's an issue when our possessions own us instead of us owning our possessions.

> Do not love this world nor the things it offers you, for
> when you love the world, you do not have the love of
> the Father in you. For the world offers only a craving for
> physical pleasure, a craving for everything we see, and
> pride in our achievements and possessions. These are not
> from the Father, but are from this world. And this world
> is fading away, along with everything that people crave.
> But anyone who does what pleases God will live forever.
> (1 John 2:15–17 NLT)

When I was praying about what God wanted me to highlight in this section, three main things came up: *status symbols, clutter,* and *shopping.* As we explore these three areas, open your heart for God to reveal any other ways in which you might cling to possessions for security. If you ask, He'll tell.

In regard to material status symbols, only you and God know if you possess something because you simply like it or because you think it secures your sense of worth. Having a nice car, a nice house, or nice clothing is not wrong or bad. But if you need people to know you have certain things, you probably derive a sense of identity from your possessions. Also, if you find yourself judging others based on the value of their possessions, or judging yourself when others have more than you, there's also an issue. You're squandering precious moments building up a false sense of identity in your mind instead of resting in your real one.

Go to God with this issue, and ask Him how to free you from the drive to seek identity and a sense of status in material things. You may be led to purge some items from your home, or simply to talk less about what you own. Or, God may direct you to do something more radical, like moving to a different town or developing a different friend group. Whom you associate with can have a huge impact on whether you base your identity in belongings—instead of the Lord.

When you stop making possessions your status symbols, you'll stop wasting time constantly trying to accumulate them or working to pay off what you've already acquired. Rather, you'll open yourself up to receive the amazing blessings God has in store for you. Sometimes those blessings actually are the physical possessions God wants you to have in your life. But more often He wants to fill your life with much richer blessings, like more peace, more joy, more love, and more laughter. Not to mention the promise of eternal life. What material things can compare to the goodness of God's ultimate gift for us? That's where I want to invest my time.

Now, about clutter: some people don't find their identity and security in the quality of items they own but in the quantity. "The more, the better" is their philosophy—even if that means having broken or unused possessions throughout their home, office, and storage areas. We can't delve into all the nuances of what might cause some people to have more cluttered lifestyles than others. Other authors have written whole books on the topic. But here are a few ways to recognize clutter as a symptom of an identity crisis in your life:

- You get a sense of security from having many posses-sions, and so you strive to fill empty spaces, perhaps even because of a poverty mentality, or fear of not having what you need in the future.
- You claim the label "messy person" as part of your identity, like a blanket excuse for not addressing the issue.
- You take comfort in being a victim of your numerous pos-sessions, particularly those inherited from family. You allow them to have power over you, instead of being able to discard them as you please. You find solace and self-protection in keeping the possessions that trap you in the past because they distract you from facing the present.

Learning how to keep your home in order is a skill, just like learning to brush your teeth. If you believe that you can learn this skill, you have accomplished the first important step toward not allowing clutter to dominate your identity.

Next, ask God to reveal what else is holding you back. If you have a fear of poverty, ask God to help you to trust Him to provide for you. And try repeating Bible verses to yourself when you're afraid of letting something go that you don't need, such as: "And my God will meet all your needs according to the riches of his glory in Christ Jesus" (Phil. 4:19).

If you've taken on the label of "messy person" in order to abdicate yourself from the responsibility to have order, ask forgiveness for taking on that false identity. Then ask God to show you who you are and what you are capable of in Christ. For example, you might pray, "I'm sorry, God, for constantly saying that 'I'm a messy person.' I'm a new creation in Christ, and I don't need to be overwhelmed by my possessions anymore. Please show me what is possible with Your help."

Finally in regard to clutter, if you hold on to items that keep your mind and heart in the past, ask God to give you the courage to mourn the past and then to let it go. We need to process the past but not take up permanent residence in it. Clinging to the past makes you a victim of it. It provides a false sense of security that keeps you from God's best for you, both now and in the future. Because if you're not willing to let go of the past, you will not free up the time, space, and energy for the new things that God wants to do in your life. This could include activities He has for you and potentially even physical moves.

As Matthew 6:19–21 says: "Do not store up for yourselves treasures on earth, where moths and vermin destroy, and where thieves break in and steal. But store up for yourselves treasures in heaven, where moths and vermin do not destroy, and where thieves do not break in and steal. For where your treasure is, there your heart will be also."

I was speaking to someone who has struggled with clutter her whole life. She has lived with her family in the same house for decades and despite saying that she wanted to get rid of stuff, had not made nearly as much progress as she would have liked. There was at least one room of her house where she dreaded even opening the door because it just felt so overwhelming.

Overall, she is an extremely smart, successful, and capable person but clutter has been a perpetual struggle. However, once she decided to stop taking on an "I'm just messy" persona, she could begin to move into a new way of living. She started to tell herself, "Decluttering is a skill, and working through areas of my home are different projects. I can take each part step-by-step and make progress. I'm not a victim of what's in my home. With God's help, I can change this part of my life." As she took on this new way of thinking, she could not only open the door of any room but also actually clean it out.

Here's where she sees herself now: "I am still not perfect, and there are still plenty of areas that need to be sorted out. But I no longer feel helpless to overcome the problem. By trusting God to teach me and lead me in this area, and not falling into the trap of believing I can change this lifelong pattern by working hard in my own strength, I am slowly but surely making progress. For me it is about having faith and God's provision."

Some people find identity and security not so much in having things but in their ability to acquire them or for others to see them buy things. This can lead to spending immense amounts of time shopping. Shopping in and of itself isn't bad. But when it keeps you from investing in more meaningful activities God wants you to do, you miss out on using your time in a way that will really satisfy your soul and bless others.

Similar to clutter, the act of shopping can further a false sense of identity and security. An unhealthy approach to shopping looks like:

- Relishing having a massive cart at checkout
- Ending up with many filled shopping bags, not because you need a lot but because you want to buy a lot
- Purchasing items you never use and may never even open
- Spending lots of time at stores with free cookies and drinks, and where salespeople spend a lot of time doting on you during an extended buying process
- Passing hours of time doing online shopping for nothing in particular—a sort of lusting after things

We'll just cover two root causes now, but God can reveal other roots of this issue to you. One possible root is that your problematic shopping simply has to do with habit. If you grew up in an environment where friends or family members did a great deal of shopping as a pastime, then acquiring more items may be a result of a way of life modeled to you. If that's the case, ask God to show you how He wants you to think about shopping and if it's something you should spend less time, energy, and resources on.

Another possible reason for over-shopping is that it's a reaction to a feeling of deprivation. Similar to how some people binge eat because they have a sense of not having had "enough" food, love, relaxation, etc., you can binge shop because of a feeling of not having enough. That could be a present reality where your shopping compensates for something you feel you lack right now. Or it could be rooted in not feeling like you could buy what you wanted or needed in the past. If this resonates with you, ask God to reveal to you the real need that you're trying to fill through shopping. Then look to Him to satisfy that deeper desire in the present, or to provide the healing from past experiences.

As Jesus says in Luke 12:15: "Watch out! Be on your guard against all kinds of greed; life does not consist in an abundance of possessions." You may have come by your shopping habit innocently. But once you know that it's distracting you from all the good that God has for you, it's time to make the choice to pull back. That means distinguishing between when you have an actual need to shop versus when you're using acquiring stuff as a way to feel better about yourself.

Breaking-Free Exercise: Possessions You Cling to for Security

You know yourself better than anyone else. I understand that this subject could make you feel super vulnerable, especially since possessions are related to our sense of security. But God wants you to be free to experience the highest quality of life possible in terms of your identity and your time. Being weighed down by the pursuit of status symbols, clutter, or over-shopping steals away your time and other resources. Plus putting security in anything other than God is idolatry.

So, to break free, be gentle but persistent. Ask God to clearly reveal the ways you may derive your security from possessions. Then request that He gives you the grace to let go. In many cases, that will simply involve a shift of heart. But at other times, it will require literally letting go of possessions so that you can be totally free to worship the Lord and have the time and space to do the things that He is calling you to do.

False Identity: Generational Patterns You Think You Need to Follow

If I hit close to home talking about possessions, then I may be slicing marrow from bone when I discuss generational patterns, or the "family way" of being or doing things.

Generational patterns impact every part of life, but for the sake of this book we'll address their impact on how you use your time. Maybe in your family, TV watching was a group habit, or working crazy hours was not only considered normal but really good. Other areas influenced by your upbringing could include how much or little sleep you get, how much time your family spends together, how much of what you do is planned—or not planned—whether or not you clean, and whether or not you get enough rest.

As if through osmosis, these patterns and ways of being were programmed into the fabric of who you are. Although you can't pick the family you grew up in, you can choose whether or not you follow the family patterns. This holds true for all people, but most especially for Christians. When we're saved, we're adopted into God's family. We have a new family tree, and we no longer need to be bound by family patterns.

> For those who are led by the Spirit of God are the children of God. The Spirit you received does not make you slaves, so that you live in fear again; rather, the Spirit you received brought about your adoption to sonship. And by him we cry, "Abba, Father."
>
> (Romans 8:14–15)

Breaking-Free Exercise: Generational Patterns You Think You Need to Follow

Think about your family. What would you say that your family is "known" for doing or not doing? How did they structure— or not structure—their days? How did they approach decisions about activities? What did they "never have time for"? Where did they maybe invest too much time? Were they always very "busy" or did they take life at a slower pace? Did they criticize people who used their time in certain ways? What did they value most with their time?

Then start to go through them one by one and ask God, "Is this right for me?" Maybe some of the ways of being match who God made you to be and are good for you to keep. But there very well may be other ways of using your time that you took on but have nothing to do with who God made you to be and wants you to be.

For those areas, it's time to let go of them as part of your identity and ask God to show you how He made you. What makes you healthy? What makes you happy? What's aligned with your true identity and purpose? It's time to stop limiting yourself by your earthly lineage and to step into all of your inheritance as a child of God.

■ ■ ■

Reflection Exercise: **BE *YOU* TIFUL**

God gave me a really cool revelation about beauty.

Basically, the world tells us if everything about our bodies is not perfect, pristine, consistent color, firmness, unlined, etc., we should despise it and try to change it. Hence many women's obsession with wrinkle creams and other beauty treatments intended to "right" what we're told is wrong about us and smash us into the latest mold.

But God has shown me that each spot, each line, each little curve where we have a little more to love is part of Him making us more and more beautiful.

As I was smiling recently and could feel the creases around my eyes, I just rejoiced in these lines, thinking that it takes a lot of smiling to make smile lines this good ☺. Isn't that cool?

Instead of seeing the process of aging as something that's making us less attractive, we can see it as something that is making us more textured, nuanced, and uniquely lovely. Aging is a natural part of God's creative process, and I'm sure He wouldn't want us to feel negative about it. Got to love God's heart toward us.

How about you? Do you see complete beauty or handsomeness in who you are, or do you find yourself struggling with the lie that you need to fit a mold, whether thinner, smoother, or younger looking?

If you're struggling, you can choose to refuse the lie that you're not enough and come into agreement with the truth that you're fearfully and wonderfully made by God.

God's best,
Elizabeth

Your beauty should not come from outward adornment, such as elaborate hairstyles and the wearing of gold jewelry or fine clothes. Rather it should be that of your inner self, the unfading beauty of a gentle and quiet spirit, which is of great worth in God's sight.

1 PETER 3:3–4

CHAPTER 4

Challenging False Beliefs

*Do not conform to the pattern of this world, but be transformed
by the renewing of your mind. Then you will be able to test
and approve what God's will is—his good, pleasing and
perfect will.*

ROMANS 12:2

God gives us exactly what we need to heal past hurts.

At a conference I attended, a speaker closed his talk with a
story about how he had been led by the Holy Spirit to buy his
adopted son a particular vintage football jersey for Christmas.
That vintage 1980 jersey was the exact one his son had been told
by foster parents that he wasn't good enough to receive. Thirty-
five years later, the adoptive father's gift of the jersey caused his
son to weep for hours. In that weeping, all of the past anger and
bitterness that had festered within him melted away, and deep
healing occurred.

I'm tenderhearted, so of course I had tears in my eyes after
hearing that testimony. And I openly received through the speaker's words that God wants to do the same healing for all of us.

A little later, I ran into a friend who also happened to be
attending the conference. She prayed for me that I would know
how much God loved me "just because."

On Tuesday of that week, I was going through some boxes in the basement and came across a piece of artwork that I had made in my hardest college class. I had managed to get an A in the class, but I had worked longer and harder than in any other college class to do so.

As I picked up the artwork—a white piece of paper showing an abstract design of geometric shapes and stippling—I sensed God tell me, "Throw that out."

I was a little taken aback by this, but I truly believe God told me again, "Throw it out."

I asked, "Why?" (Maybe not the most reverent thing to do, but I wanted to understand.)

"I hated what that class did to you," He replied. "I hated all the sleep you lost, the striving, the focusing on creating whatever your professor wanted you to create to make the grade, instead of creating what was authentic to you. Throw it out."

So I did . . .

Later that night, I had dinner with the friend who had prayed for me the previous Sunday night at the conference. She repeated that God wanted me to know that I was loved and He would do anything for me, "just because."

The next morning, I opened my e-mail, and the subject line, "Just Because {Encouragement for Today}" caught my eye.

I clicked on it and read a Proverbs 31 Ministries newsletter piece written by Lysa TerKeurst.[8] It started out with this verse:

> Dear children, let's not merely say that we love each
> other; let us show the truth by our actions.
>
> (1 John 3:18 NLT)

---

[8] Lysa TerKeurst, "Just Because," Proverbs 31 newsletter, January 27, 2016.

Then it went on to tell the beautiful story of a couple named Grace and Jim who had been together for forty-two years. And on the seventeenth day of every month, Jim would do something loving for Grace, "just because." Those mementos could include a note or flowers or some other kind gesture, but the note was always "just because" to remind Grace that his love was unconditional—no matter what.

And on the seventeenth of the first month after Jim passed away, a letter arrived to Grace with this inscription:

Not even death shall stop my heart. Just because, Jim.

Jim had arranged with the postman to deliver it on just the right day so Grace would know she was always remembered, always loved, always chosen, just because...

I completely broke down in tears. (I promise I don't cry all the time, but the best God stories usually involve tissues.) Not just because this was a touching story of a beautiful marriage. But because this was God's answer to what had been spoken on Sunday night of bringing the past into the present and healing something deep within me. This was my vintage football jersey.

As I wept, God spoke to my heart. He told me how what I thought were amazing achievements—like getting straight As from middle school through college, or giving a graduation speech before thousands as a valedictorian—had been bittersweet for Him. I believe God was happy that I felt achievement. But He grieved what it had cost me as His daughter. I pushed so hard to make the grade, lost sleep, tried to please people instead of being in a relationship with them, and most of all, I lost the sense that I was enough just for being me.

Really, God always has and always will love me "just because."

He wants me to love others and myself with this same sort of abandon, with love free from performance expectations.

Many of the things we glory in, God showed me make Him weep. He weeps over executives in corner offices, trying to numb the burden of their relentless workload and the impossible expectations imposed upon them with excesses of all sorts...

He weeps over the stay-at-home moms who cry at night because they're trying so hard to be the perfect wife, the perfect mother, have the perfect house, and look perfect but never feel like they measure up.

He weeps over the Olympics. It's an amazing honor, and the ultimate dream of many athletes to represent their country. But the glory undeniably comes at a cost. Many lives and families are strained, and bodies are torn apart. At the end of the time, for what? A slice of metal.

God's greatest joy is seeing you at rest. Seeing you throw back your head and give a big, deep-down laugh, and roll around on the floor a bit while you're at it.

Just because...

■　■　■

WHY WE NEED TO LIVE FROM IDENTITY NOT FOR IDENTITY

Letting go of the false identities we talked about in the last chapter can feel horribly vulnerable. It can set you adrift and make you feel like you have nothing to be proud of. It can make you feel naked, unprotected, and even like you are going to die. It's a sad, sad thing that some people no longer feel like living when they lose their jobs, their businesses, their fortunes, their relationships, or whatever else they believed made them "them."

You may be thinking, "If this is the case, Elizabeth, why in the world would you be encouraging me to let go??!! Life is pretty good as it is; there's no need to screw things up."

To clarify, I'm not encouraging you to purposely screw anything up. It's wonderful for you to have success at work, enjoy where you live, and be in good relationships. It's just extremely dangerous for you to form your sense of self around temporal, earthly things that may come and may go.

God wants you to be totally free. God wants you to enter into all He has for you. That's only possible when your core identity is centered in Him and nothing else. As I was praying about this chapter, God told me that changing how you think about your identity is the most important thing that could happen to you after being saved. Because when you know your true identity in Christ and "live from identity instead of for identity" as Eric Allen, a pastor at Bethel Church, says, all things become possible.[9]

One of the biggest reasons so many of us struggle in this area is that the false beliefs that encouraged us to form and hold on to false identities are very convincing. They seem so real and so natural that it's hard to believe they're false. In fact, unless we stop and consciously challenge them, we will keep believing what the world says, instead of believing in what God says, is the truth about our identity.

---

[9] This was from a Bethel Breakout session I attended on April 18, 2016, in Royal Oak, Michigan.

★ ★ ★

Three of the fundamental paradigm shifts we need to have in relation to identity are:

- Uncertain vs. certain
- External vs. internal
- Relative vs. absolute

The lie from the world is that you always need to measure up. If you don't—watch out. The truth from God is that in Christ your identity is certain. It has been established and there's nothing you can do to achieve more or less in it.

The lie from the world is that what you possess externally, such as money, houses, positions, or relationships, determines your identity. The truth from God is that what you possess *internally* determines who you are.

The lie from the world is that your identity is relative to the people around you—are they "better" or "worse" than you in some way? Do they approve or not approve of you? The truth from God is that your identity is absolute and the judgments of men and comparison simply don't matter to Him.

Once you've identified these lies, then you can challenge them using the techniques described in this chapter. With God's help you can be set free to discover and love your true identity. When you love who you are and let go of false identities, you free up a massive amount of time you'd be spending trying to earn what you already have—unconditional love and acceptance. This in turn allows you to invest your time in a way that leads to the very best God has for you in every area of your life.

THE ESSENTIAL PARADIGM SHIFTS

Essential Shift: Uncertain vs. Certain

In an ideal world, you receive exactly what you need from your parents and everyone else around you, from the time you were conceived to the present day, to feel unconditionally loved and accepted. This builds a deep sense of security inside of you, a knowing that you are enough, and a belief that you are worthy of love and belonging.

Because this world is less than ideal—thank you, Adam and Eve—even when we have great parents, many of us don't build a deep-down certainty in our true identity as a child. We face experiences that inhibit our sense of security, or our flawed interpretation of experiences does this. Lack of security in our attachment to our primary caregivers leads to an adulthood lived according to fear bonds instead of love bonds.

The book *Living from the Heart Jesus Gave You* takes an in-depth look at the differences between love bonding and fear bonding styles in relationships. But a few key differences I'll contrast here are that with love bonds, the fundamental question when deciding what to do is "How do I act like myself?" and the bonds between you and others are "based on love and characterized by truth, closeness, intimacy, joy, peace, perseverance, and authentic giving."[10]

With fear bonds the core question is, "How do I get what I want?" and the bonds are "based on fear and characterized by

---

[10] James G. Friesen et al., *Living from the Heart Jesus Gave You* (East Peoria, IL: Shepherd's House Inc., 2013), 69.

pain, humiliation, desperation, shame, guilt, and/or fear of rejection, abandonment, or detrimental consequences."[11]

As part of developing certainty in our identity, we need to develop love bonds with God, with others, and with ourselves. This takes us away from the sense that we're never quite sure where we stand—where we constantly question our place in the world—to a place of deep certainty in our coherent sense of self.

When you feel uncertain about your core identity, it can make you feel afraid whenever you feel like you might not measure up. This fear-based way of being was entwined in my DNA for many years, so much that I couldn't recognize that it really wasn't me. But as God has healed me, the fear comes less and less often, and the sense of it being OK to be just me has grown tremendously.

For example, early in my career, I'd get so afraid to make a mistake on anything. I would apologize profusely and obsess over what I had done wrong and how I never wanted it to happen again. Fast-forward to the present. Now, of course, I still try to avoid mistakes, but I also accept that they will happen. Occasionally, I misspell something, call someone the wrong name, or get the time of a meeting wrong.

Because of my growth in unconditional self-acceptance, I can now laugh mistakes off pretty easily and tell myself and others that "oops! moments" are good reminders that I'm human. The growing certainty in my identity—that I'm OK no matter what happens—literally saves me hours of time worrying about making a blunder or fretting if I do make one. Plus, quite frankly, this new way of being helps me relate to others with more ease.

---

[11] Ibid.

People who try to be perfect can be kind of annoying. I can say that because I've been one.

It's good to calm down about life and have a healthier, more balanced way of thinking. And ultimately, the means of us having an unshakable sense of certainty in our identity is the Lord. To be secure in who we are, we must choose to believe what God tells us over what we've heard or believed in the past. Then we can stop questioning whether or not we're enough and start abiding in God's love.

These techniques can open you up to a deeper and deeper certainty in your identity in Christ.

Read and Believe the Word: One of the most important aims when doing this is to soak yourself in the truth of what God's Word says about your identity. Here are a few select verses, but you can find many, many more by searching online for "Who I am in Christ." Repeat these to yourself often, especially when you're feeling discouraged, and put them up in places you can see them:

> For we are God's handiwork, created in Christ Jesus to do good works, which God prepared in advance for us to do.
>
> (Ephesians 2:10)

> So in Christ Jesus you are all children of God through faith.
>
> (Galatians 3:26)

> Therefore, as God's chosen people, holy and dearly loved, clothe yourselves with compassion, kindness, humility, gentleness and patience.
>
> (Colossians 3:12)

In all these things we are more than conquerors through
him who loved us. For I am convinced that neither death
nor life, neither angels nor demons, neither the present
nor the future, nor any powers, neither height nor depth,
nor anything else in all creation, will be able to separate
us from the love of God that is in Christ Jesus our Lord.

(Romans 8:37–39)

Listen to the Truth: The Word of God is a powerful force that
can transform your life (see Heb. 4:12). During times when I
needed to do some major reprogramming of my brain to focus
on the truth of who I am, listening to the Word has been really
helpful. You can find resources on YouTube with encouraging
verses, record your own affirmations of who you are in Christ, or
purchase recordings that help reinforce the truth of God's Word
about your sound identity in Him. In my process of healing, I
found the affirmations CDs from the Ultimate Journey ministry very helpful: www.theultimatejourney.org/store/phase-1
/phase-1-affirmation-cd/. I would listen to them again and again
to help remind me of the truth of my identity in Christ. I also
found the "Rise Up a Warrior" soaking session from Graham
Cooke encouraging when I went through a time where I felt
really discouraged. It helped me to accept the truth of who I was
in Christ and fight back against the enemy's attack on my identity: www.brilliantbookhouse.com/rise-up-a-warrior.

Allow God to Transform You: Ultimately, this is a process.
I've consciously been working on repatterning my beliefs about
myself since 2007. Since beliefs lead to emotions, which lead to
behaviors, I know I need to focus on right beliefs about who I am
in order to have right behaviors. One of the biggest new-to-me

and yet oh-so-true beliefs I needed to allow God to integrate into my core sense of identity is that it's the *most logical and reasonable thing in the world to believe that I'm worthy of unconditional love, acceptance, and care.* God could have made humans like some animals who can survive on their own from the moment they are born. But He didn't. Instead, God created people to be completely dependent on years of unconditional love and care from individuals who had never met them before and at a point when they were incapable of consciously giving their caregivers anything back. Nature points to the truth that every individual is worthy of unconditional love and care. And God can give us the grace to accept this truth at a deep level, no matter what some of our experiences may have led us to believe.

I appreciate that I need to participate as God works in me, but only God can completely heal me of all insecurity. When I'm struggling with uncertainty about my identity, I can choose to believe that, despite my emotions at any time, I am 100 percent secure in Christ. Doing this prevents me from using my time in a fear-driven way and opens me up to receive God's direction.

When I know that my core identity is certain, I have total freedom to do or not do anything in my life without fear of loss of identity, including day-to-day tasks as well as big-picture commitments.

■   ■   ■

Essential Shift: External vs. Internal

To support your true sense of identity, you need to shift from an external sense of self to an internal one. This involves not only letting go of all of the false labels, molds, and attributes discussed in the last chapter but also shifting your attention from the outside world to your internal world.

I've realized that very often when you feel insecure, the answer is not to do more or do better. Instead, the answer is to focus on unconditional love and acceptance of yourself. Most times you feel insecure, the issue is within you not outside of you. You don't need to prove your worth but instead accept it and receive it in Christ.

> *If you're not sure if you're insecure, pay attention to how you judge others. Your judgment of others typically points to your own insecurity.*

One of my former Divine Time Management group coaching members, Jacques Michael Casparian, put it so well:

> Trying to attain security through performance is generally as ineffective as hiding behind fig leaves—it places a Band-Aid on much bigger issues of guilt and shame. Instead we need to trust in the unconditional love of our heavenly Father as we humbly "ask, seek, and knock" with focused intentionality. Then, after we find acceptance by realizing "whose" we are, and what it means to be created in His image, we can begin to live life to the fullest and truly love God and our neighbor as ourselves.[12]

And Tim Tebow, professional baseball player, former professional football player, author of *Shaken: Discovering Your True Identity in the Midst of Life's Storms*, and devoted follower of Christ, shared similar sentiments in a Proverbs 31 Ministry

---

[12] Jacques Michael Casparian, Facebook post, October 6, 2016.

newsletter on "Knowing Whose You Are Changes Everything." In it, he expressed that we need to avoid society's pressure to allow external things, like our car, our bank balance, or our looks, define us because none of the material stuff lasts. Instead, he encourages us all to ground ourselves in our identity in Jesus Christ and to remember whose we are: "We are children of God. We were created by Love, in love and for love."[13]

Trading an external sense of identity for an internal one is really tough—we can only do this with God's help. From the time you were born, if not before, you've been measured and monitored. From day one your height and weight have been on display. Welcome to the world, baby girl or baby boy, let's show your stats so people can start judging whether you're "normal" or not in comparison to others. And the charts and measuring sticks only increase with age, from grades at school to scoreboards on the field.

Of course it's natural and normal for there to be some monitoring of our lives so that our parents can help us grow and mature in a healthy way mentally, physically, emotionally, and spiritually. But can you see how ingrained this sense of an external "score" is in our cultural mind-set? And can you see how it could cause you to look outside yourself instead of inside yourself to God to know that you're OK and enough?

The basic premise behind an external sense of identity is: "If I meet or have this [external measure of success or achievement], then I have identity and I'm enough." The converse is also true:

---

[13] Tim Tebow, Proverbs 31 Ministries newsletter, "Knowing Whose You Are Changes Everything," October 26, 2016.

"If I don't meet or have this [underline: external measure of success or achievement], then I don't have identity and I'm not enough. Therefore I should invest my time, energy, and resources to get this external sense of self."

This wrong mind-set takes away our ability to truly invest our time in what is best for us because we're driven by fear. This can lead to feeling an overwhelming compulsion to do or not do certain things because we "need" to in order to get certain external results to feel OK with ourselves. I believe this is one of the biggest barriers most people have standing in the way of having time to rest and feeling at peace.

As God is pulling me more and more out of the world, He's shown me how dangerous it is to our sense of self and relationship with Him to base identity on any of the things of this world.

> Do not love the world or anything in the world. If anyone
> loves the world, love for the Father is not in them. For
> everything in the world—the lust of the flesh, the lust of
> the eyes, and the pride of life—comes not from the Father
> but from the world. The world and its desires pass away,
> but whoever does the will of God lives forever.
>
> (1 John 2:15–17)

I understand there's a time and place for trackers such as Fitbit. If they make you healthier and happier, awesome! I'm an advocate of sleep and exercise. But I'm also a voice of dissent against focusing too much on external measurements, especially when you let it impact how you feel about your identity.

In my *Harvard Business Review* digital article, "The Perils of Overmonitoring Your Behavior and Goals," I share these insights:

Overmonitoring can have dire consequences. Instead of living life, they make life a test: Did I wake up on time? Am I answering everyone's emails in an acceptable time period? How do all of my numbers look? Did I estimate all of my to-dos for the day accurately? Did I eat the diet du jour that's supposed to give me the most energy while still being environmentally friendly? Did I...? Did I...? Did I...?

These individuals have an internal monitor that's always on, regulating the actions of the external façade that they believe is "right" or "appropriate." On the positive side, these people tend to get a steady stream of affirmation for being so responsible, dependable, and predictable. After all, they're seemingly getting all their work done while meeting the needs of others. But by putting so much emphasis on what others want—or even what they just think others want—they are not being true to their own priorities. That always-on, always-perfect, always-positive front can cause them to lose their connection to themselves and to others.

I've been that person. And in my experience, the greatest risk of this overmonitored life is losing track of yourself. If you're overly concerned about doing what is "right," you can misplace your sense of what you actually want, think, and like (or don't like).[14]

---

[14] Elizabeth Grace Saunders, "The Perils of Overmonitoring Your Behavior and Goals," *Harvard Business Review* digital article, February 19, 2016, https://hbr.org/2016/02/the-perils-of-overmonitoring-your-behavior-and-goals.

So how do we do life differently than the world expects and have our identity focused on what's internally true about us, not all the externals? Here are a few strategies that can help you partner with God in this transition.

Be Willing to Let Go: Depending on where you fall on the spectrum in various aspects of life, you will legitimately need to do more or less monitoring. If you're diabetic, please keep track of your eating and blood sugar, and if you're someone who struggles to pay your bills, recording and watching your expenses is a wise move. I'm not insinuating that you should let go of all responsibility. If you have certain areas where you need to be vigilant to stay healthy and be a good steward, I pray God encourages you in those disciplines. But for those who tend to overmonitor, it's time to loosen up and stop keeping as much track of externals.

For example, I am careful to avoid looking at numbers in my business too often. I am very blessed that my business is doing well. But I don't constantly check the number of shares or comments on my posts, the number of books I sell, or even my revenue numbers. I find it's best for my soul to focus on serving from the heart and not to look for constant external validation. This not only saves me time doing checks that don't actually change the numbers but also gives me more time to invest in doing the work that will benefit my business and, Lord willing, touch people's lives.

Be Honest about the Why: It is possible to be attractive, be successful in your job, have a beautiful home and fantastic relationships and not derive your identity from these external things. It's also possible to be kind of average in a lot of areas and to strongly put your identity in externals instead of in God. No one can really tell by outward appearances, only you and God know what's going on in your heart (see 1 Sam. 16:7).

You don't need to live in poverty, downplay your appearance, or pretend that you're not as fantastic as you are. That's false humility. It's not pride to accept the reality of who God made you. You're His masterpiece—this is just as true even if you don't have a vibrant career, movie star looks, or many close relationships. The point is, you are wonderful because you are made in His image. So, no matter what your external circumstances, you can be very proud of who you are internally.

Do a heart check with yourself in regard to externals to discern the "why." This will help you evaluate whether you are spending your time according to God's desires for you. Are you living as you're living because it's authentic to who you are and makes you happy? Or are these your motivating factors:

- Feeling better than other people
- Fitting in (at least externally)
- Other people admiring you
- Getting a positive reaction from people
- Fear you'll be rejected or not be enough

My heart's desire for you is that you will receive and experience all the abundance God has for you but never base your identity on the external.

Accept Blessings with Humble Gratitude: Proverbs 10:22 tells us: "The blessing of the LORD makes a person rich, and He adds no sorrow with it" (NLT). I believe you can substitute any other good thing for the word *rich* in that verse, such as *have good relationships*, or *healthy*. I find that when I stop grasping for things

God is not giving me and instead wait to receive His goodness, I get the good stuff without a bad aftertaste.

Also, when I don't grasp and strive for things, I know it was God and not me who gave me whatever I have or enabled my accomplishments. My response to these positive externals, like amazing friends or success in my business, is then to simply be grateful. I know it's all blessings from the Lord and my response is not "yeah me" but "yeah God!"

I do encourage you to try to enjoy the external reminders of God's goodness, from being healthy to living in a beautiful, orderly home. But you're not defined by those things, and I don't want you to worry about what people think about who you are or what you have. I just want you to be at peace knowing your identity is internal and in God, you're enough.

■ ■ ■

Essential Shift: Relative vs. Absolute

When you write a book with a lot of truth in it, it feels like you're putting one of those magnifying mirrors up to your face. Let's be honest, the reflection is not always so pretty. You see wrinkles and little hairs you never saw in normal light or with regular mirrors. All of a sudden you feel like you need to book an appointment at the salon—ASAP.

This last section of this chapter feels especially like that for me right now. I prayed to God about how honest I should be with you about some of my struggles, and I feel guided to share it all. So I will. My heart's desire is that sharing my truth will set you free. I hope you won't judge me for not being perfect. But if you do, I already forgive you and bless you in advance.

Identity being relative versus absolute is about whether you answer yes to the first or the second of these questions: *Do I see my identity as something that is about who I am or what I have in comparison to the people around me? Or do I see my identity as something that is fixed and not better or worse depending on who I am around?*

Comparison is rooted in self-absorption and insecurity, and fosters a tendency to look past people to see your own reflection in the mirror behind them. This can lead to wasting a great deal of time judging other people and worrying about what other people think of you versus simply living your life to the full.

Ultimately, you need to be present with people and have the eyes of your heart focused on the Lord, not yourself. Only God can be the perfect reflection of your true identity.

This is a tricky area for me, one where I've grown a lot but still struggle sometimes, especially since I'm naturally bent toward being an achiever. As we've discussed previously, the world tells us from a young age that we need to have a certain rank to be OK, to have identity and in turn be safe and loved. But that's not God's way.

Here's what God says:

> Do nothing out of selfish ambition or vain conceit.
> Rather, in humility value others above yourselves, not looking to your own interests but each of you to the interests of the others.
>
> (Philippians 2:3–4)

> When he noticed how the guests picked the places of honor at the table, he told them this parable: "When

someone invites you to a wedding feast, do not take the place of honor, for a person more distinguished than you may have been invited. If so, the host who invited both of you will come and say to you, 'Give this person your seat.' Then, humiliated, you will have to take the least important place. But when you are invited, take the lowest place, so that when your host comes, he will say to you, 'Friend, move up to a better place.' Then you will be honored in the presence of all the other guests. For all those who exalt themselves will be humbled, and those who humble themselves will be exalted."

(Luke 14:7–11)

I like to believe that most of the time I do live out these ideals that God extols, so my identity in Christ can feel absolute, not relative. I don't tend to get envious if people have bigger, nicer houses than me. I don't get bent out of shape if someone has a bigger business than I do, or has a more visible role in the church than I have. Overall I feel pretty good about who I am.

But there are some areas where I still struggle sometimes. Even though I'm objectively an in-shape, attractive person, I sometimes find myself questioning if I'm as pretty as the other women around me. I've even felt insecure and compared my body to instructors in workout videos. I know that sounds absolutely ridiculous given that I'll never meet these people and their whole job is to be in awesome shape. But I'll admit it still happens occasionally. I'm so grateful that God is healing and freeing me of this so it happens less and less.

Also, in general, I don't compare my work to others'. But there are certain situations when I can feel particularly vulnerable.

For example, whenever I have a new book come out, I can struggle with comparing myself to the other people launching a book at the same time. I can worry that I'm not doing as much as them or selling as many books as they have sold. Sometimes I need to unsubscribe from their newsletters because it is too distracting to look at what they're doing and then constantly ask myself if I'm measuring up.

These and other areas are ones in which God is still doing His refining work in my life. When "ego threats" arise, meaning that how someone is doing in a particular area has a high level of relevance to me as well as a high level of closeness,[15] I need to turn to the Lord and say, "Help!" and take these steps.

Turn to God for Deliverance: When you start to feel envious, jealous, or insecure, you can ask God to show you how there is enough love, attention, respect, and resources for you as well as everyone else in the world and that another person's success is not your failure. This is true even when it may appear that there is a competition for finite resources, like interviewing for the same job as a colleague. You want a heavenly abundance mind-set not an earthly poverty mind-set. You can also ask God to help you to see that you get to be yourself and other people get to be themselves, and you can rejoice in the good in both your lives. Our value is absolute for all of us.

Guard Your Heart: Be aware of your limits. If you need to avoid certain situations that could cause you pain, that's OK. It's natural to need to stay away from some events, conversations, or social media when you're particularly emotionally vulnerable.

---

[15] Heidi Grant Halvorson, *No One Understands You and What to Do About It* (Boston: Harvard Business Review Press, 2015), 110–111.

You don't need to tempt yourself to sin. It's wise to know how much you can handle.

Refrain from Gossip: Finally, it's good to be completely honest and transparent with God about the ugliness inside because He can clean it up. But please don't go around talking to other people about it. That leads to gossip, hurt feelings, and more envy, jealousy, and insecurity. When you have an issue with being insecure and putting your identity as relative to someone else, that's not the other person's problem. It's yours.

It's time for us to open up our hearts to the Lord to allow Him to do the surgery to make us completely, absolutely, totally secure in Him regardless of what's happening with anyone else.

Our identity and place in the world are completely unique. The truth that we are totally accepted and loved is absolute in God.

My prayer for you and for me is that all of us will go through these essential paradigm shifts so that we can live life from a place of certainty in our internal, absolute identity in God. In Jesus' name. Amen.

We've talked a lot about what not to do. In the next chapter, we'll be exploring what it looks like to discover and love our true identities. In doing so, we then have the freedom to use our time and energy in alignment with God's best.

■　■　■

Reflection Exercise: **STOP PUSHING**

Sometimes we unnecessarily deprive ourselves of all God desires us to have in our lives because of how we feel we need to measure up.

For example, in high school I developed the tendency of over-working. In retrospect, I know that there were times when I could have allowed myself to go outside and have fun playing with my siblings or could have spent more time with friends. But because I was so stuck in the mentality that I needed to be responsible and achieve certain things to get into college and get scholarships, I didn't allow myself that time.

I've come a long way since then and have much more down-time and social time. But sometimes the lie that I need to work so hard to get everything done still pops up. I find that it is especially strong when I'm feeling insecure, because being busy or working is a convenient way for me to numb out and feel like I don't need anyone.

I got sideswiped by this wrong way of thinking recently. God in His kindness showed me how much He loves me, how much He wants me to rest, and how much joy He has in me doing what I love and spending time with people I love. I realized I need to remember to give myself permission to pay attention to my feelings. There are times when I need to push through at work—like on a weekday afternoon when I'm just having an energy slump. But there are also many times when I need to say—wait—I'm feeling isolated, tired, or dis-connected. I need to honor my feelings and get what I need whether that is a nap, some prayer time, or some connection with people.

Has this ever happened to you? Do you ever find yourself put-ting more and more into your schedule so that you can block out concerns, people, and sometimes even God? If so, I encourage you to remember that God is a God of tenderness, gentleness, and love. He calls us sons and daughters and doesn't want us to live as slaves to anything or anyone but Christ.

If you're open to it, I encourage you to take these steps:

- Think about any ways in which you might be pushing yourself harder than you need to. Or maybe you're not pushing yourself really hard but you're not giving your heart and soul what they crave. One red flag is when you have to do a lot of self-talk to convince yourself that whatever you're depriving yourself of is worth it.

- Then I want you to consider why you are overriding your needs. Is it about fear that you need to make everything happen on your own instead of trusting in God? Is it about feeling vulnerable that if you ask for what you need that you might not get it—like reaching out to a friend to get together?

- Finally, I want you to ask God to show you how you can honor your needs this week. So often some of the smallest things like taking a short walk on a beautiful day, taking time to read, having a good conversation, or spending a few hours with people who love and support you can make all the difference in the world.

May you always know that you are valued and precious and God deeply longs for you to live a life of peace, joy, and abundance of all good things.

God's best,
Elizabeth

> *But now, this is what the* Lord *says—*
> *he who created you, Jacob,*
> *he who formed you, Israel:*
> *"Do not fear, for I have redeemed you;*
> *I have summoned you by name; you are mine."*

Isaiah 43:1

CHAPTER 5

Discovering Your True Identity

And we all, who with unveiled faces contemplate the Lord's glory, are being transformed into his image with ever-increasing glory, which comes from the Lord, who is the Spirit.

2 CORINTHIANS 3:18

"Everyone loves Elizabeth" was one of my beliefs up through mid-2015.

Because of my tendency to know how to present to others what I believed they wanted to see, I actually thought this could be true 99 percent of the time. And I feared whenever someone didn't like me, because that meant something was wrong with the other person—or worse yet, me.

This tendency to base my way of being on popular opinion did lead to me having quite the extensive friend network and little to no conflict or awkwardness. But it also led to a somewhat fragmented and confused sense of self.

It was hard to tell what was really "me" versus what I believed others or even society at large wanted me to be.

It also led to me sometimes choosing to do things I felt I should do but that stressed me out, such as being friends with certain people who made me uncomfortable to "be nice" or taking on certain work projects I dreaded because it "made sense."

★ ★ ★

God in His mercy put me on a nine-month rebirth process from late July 2015 through April 30, 2016.

May 1, 2016, was my "rebirth" date.

By the time that I got to that date, I had come to terms with the fact that not everyone loved Elizabeth, and that was OK. I loved Elizabeth—the real, true, authentic Elizabeth;

The Elizabeth who is tenderhearted, and yet has good boundaries and can freely choose whom she does and does not spend time with.

The Elizabeth who is bold and confident in the Lord and sings really loud at church and sometimes dances too.

The Elizabeth who loves to hike but doesn't prefer to camp.

The Elizabeth who is a beloved child of God, just like all Christians, and yet is also unique and different in her own special way.

The Elizabeth who thrives in flitting around large crowds of people and yet deeply treasures her quiet time each morning alone with the Lord.

The Elizabeth who has a special calling and destiny to shine as a light for the Lord, which right now includes writing her first Christian inspiration book.

The Elizabeth who recognizes that being loved by God and aligned with her eternal purpose is far more important than popularity ratings.

And so much more...

I find that being true to my true identity has led to a greater congruence, greater peace, greater flow, and less second-guessing. I also find that I have fewer relationship, but they are more deeply satisfying. I'm not trying to fit in meeting with everyone that I could or doing everything that I could. That causes me to feel less stretched for time and pressured. That gives me time to breathe. It also gives me the time to be present and to truly enjoy whatever activity I'm doing at the moment.

I now love "me," and I love being the *me* who God created me to be.

My prayer for you is that through this chapter you'll receive greater insight into what it means to be the true "you."

■　■　■

THE MAGNIFICENT UNVEILING

The best news about learning to know and love your true identity is that you don't have to figure anything out on your own. The greatest expert on who you are and what you're created to do knows you and loves you and wants to tell you.

God is very creative so He can reveal your identity in any way He chooses: from dramatic ways like talking to you from a burning bush, sending someone to anoint you as king (if you live in a country with those sorts of offices), or having an angel come talk to you. Or, He can talk to you in simple-yet-deeply-intimate moments: when you're sitting on rocks overlooking a lake, and the wind brushes your cheek and you know in that instant that you're exactly where you're supposed to be and who you're supposed to be. Or when you're reading the Word and all of a sudden, it seems like God pulled out a highlighter and a particular verse jumps off the page. You know it's for you.

Each person is incredibly unique, and I believe how God communicates in each situation is incredibly unique. So I do not want to have the foolishness to put what God will do in a box.

But as a general rule, you can gain revelation about your true identity from these types of sources:

- The Word
- The Spirit
- The body
- The anointing

First, God's Word is living and active and powerful. It can speak to you about the truth of your identity in Christ as a child of God and citizen of God's kingdom. Much of what you read in the Bible will be universally applicable to all Christians. But sometimes God will highlight particular verses or a certain story to show you something unique about you that may not apply to others.

Second, I believe that God can and does communicate with us directly. We won't go into any deep theological discussion here. But many people would call this communicating with the Holy Spirit. Through this Spirit, we can hear God's voice, sense His presence, see spiritual realities, and have Him speak to us in other ways such as dreams.

Third, although people-pleasing is not a good idea, listening to what wise people who know your heart say about who you are is a helpful way to discover your true self. When people are accurate mirrors, what they say rings true. You might even think to yourself, "I hadn't really even thought about the fact that I do this or that until you mentioned it, it's just me being me."

Finally, if you've been called, anointed, or chosen for a certain position or role, that can give insight into a part of your identity for a certain season. Sometimes this will be obvious through God showing you to do something or having you chosen for something big. Other times it will be subtle, where you volunteer for an activity or simply decide to start moving forward on your own. It's wise to be discerning when people ask you to do something and to avoid automatically assuming what they asked you to do is your calling. Sometimes it's the Lord communicating through them and other times it's not. Consider every opportunity in prayer.

Throughout this chapter, we'll look at different ways in which these four areas can reveal more and more of the true you. When you know and love the true you, you can make decisions about your time aligned with God's best.

> As you go through the process of discovering your true identity, it's imperative to be open to discovering the real you. At NorthRidge Church, Pastor Jason Miller did a powerful teaching on overcoming the power of shame. You can watch the full sermon here: http://northridgechurch.com/experience/talks/jason-miller/217/.[16]
>
> Jason makes many great points in his talk. But one that I believe is most essential to us here is this: shame is a liar and takes something good about you and says that it's bad. You are who you are for a reason. God doesn't make mistakes. When we stop hiding our "flaws," we often find that they're in fact where our greatest strength and most stunning beauty lie.

[16] Jason Miller, "Jason Miller Unforgettable 2017" (sermon at NorthRidge Church, Plymouth, Michigan, July 9, 2017), http://northridgechurch.com/experience/talks/jason-miller/217/.

SOURCES OF INSIGHT

Source of Insight: The Word

> *For the word of God is alive and active. Sharper than any*
> *double-edged sword, it penetrates even to dividing soul and*
> *spirit, joints and marrow; it judges the thoughts and attitudes*
> *of the heart.*
>
> HEBREWS 4:12

I grew up in a church that put a big emphasis on studying the Bible, so during sermons we would flip all over the place. And I also had the blessing of growing up in a home with two parents who made their faith a priority, including reading the Word on a daily basis. In a large part because of their example starting at about the time I was eleven years old, I began reading the Bible myself each morning. When I was at home, that looked like my dad being on one end of the living room couch with his Bible and journal, and me being on the other end of the couch with my Bible and journal. Then it transitioned to me reading my Bible at the college cafeteria in the morning, and now it looks like me sitting at my own dining room table, reading during breakfast. I love and cherish this time. In fact, I feel very uncomfortable if I don't have it because it's so centering for me.

Because of this heritage of being in the Bible, I have many Scriptures entwined in my spirit. I can't necessarily tell you where they are all located in the Word, but I generally can give a pretty good paraphrase. I'm also quite familiar with reading the Bible. I feel comfortable with it and understand it.

I know that's not true for everyone, so when I suggest that you find your true identity by reading the Bible, your eyes may kind of glaze over. If that's you, hang in there with me. You don't need to get overwhelmed. I've got some helpful tips for you coming up.

And I encourage you to give finding your true identity in the Word a try, because in many ways the Bible is the easiest way to hear from God. It's written and very tangible so you don't need to question if you're hearing from God, yourself, or some other influence. You know the source.

Also it's good to know that there's no one right way to spend time in the Word and definitely no one right way to find your identity in it. But here are some ideas of how to start hearing God's voice about who you are through the Bible. In doing so, you can live out of your true identity, including making choices aligned with His best with your time.

Start Anywhere: Don't worry about being perfect with reading the Bible. You don't need to be a Greek or Hebrew scholar, and you don't even need to understand everything that you're reading. If you're struggling with something and do want to understand more, you can look up what are called "commentaries" online. Another alternative is to use a study Bible or a devotional, which will help you gain understanding through the Scriptures. You can also read The Message version of the Bible. This version of the Word is not highly technically accurate in terms of the translation but can give you a general sense of what the passages mean in modern-day terms. I read a Bible that has the New American Standard Bible version on one side of the page, which is a more literal translation of the Bible, and The Message version on the other side of the page so they are side by side. Finally, you can do things like look up online "What does the Bible say about my identity?" or "What does the Bible say about who I am in Christ?" This will take you to lists of Bible verses to read through. All of the verses can be helpful, but there may be ones in particular that really speak to your spirit.

Make It a Habit: In Matthew 4:4, "Jesus answered, 'It is written: "Man shall not live on bread alone, but on every word that comes from the mouth of God." ' " Just like we need to eat food every day to stay healthy, we need to have the Bible as part of our lives every day to stay spiritually nourished. As you spend more time reading the Word, God can speak to you more through it about your identity. You may find that a particular person in the Bible really inspires you and that God tells you that you have a similar calling in life as that person. Or you may simply realize more and more of your true identity as you see more and more of who God is and how He loves you. I recommend incorporating reading the Bible into your morning routine right when you get up or your bedtime routine right before you fall asleep because that increases your chances of being consistent. (Of course if you have an alternate time that already works for you—stick with it!)

I have my Bible and journals on my nightstand. Before I leave my bedroom in the morning, I pick them up and immediately bring them to the dining room table. I then prop my bottle of multivitamins under my Bible to get it in position for me to read while I eat breakfast.

Be Open: In my experience, God doesn't follow a formula where if you do X and Y, then you get Z answer. He's very relationship oriented, so He wants you to stay close to Him and do what He says step-by-step. So for example, you may be reading a devotional about your identity in Christ and then all of a sudden have the strong feeling that you should stop and read something else in the Bible. If so, go for it. God might have something else to teach you about who you are in Christ that wasn't in the devotional. Or you may be reading through a particular book of the Bible and then open up to a different passage one morning and realize God had something significant for you there. Keep asking God to speak to you about your identity through His Word, and He will answer. Sometimes that will be telling you how much He loves you. Other times it will be helping you understand how you're called to relate to others. And in other instances it may be a harder word around being someone who needs to take up your cross. All these things are true about your identity. God just highlights what we need to focus on in different ways at different times.

Write Down What Strikes You: Some people like to write or highlight in their Bibles. If that's you, you may want to come up with a special symbol or color that indicates it's something God is showing you about your identity in Him, either in general as a Christian or in particular in regard to yourself. I'm not a writing-in-the-Bible type of gal, so I tend to list my insights in my journal. When I'm working on hearing something in particular from the Lord, I'll have a special page near the back of my journal where I'll write down everything that comes to me. So if I wanted to understand more of my true identity, I would have a page labeled "True Identity" at the top. Then anytime a verse or phrase or word struck me from the Bible, I would write it down on that page. If you're not a journal-carrying person like me, you can write the insights God gives you on your true identity on a paper you stick in your Bible or a note on your phone, if you're more into digital Bibles. And if you really love a verse, hang it up on your wall or put it somewhere else where you'll see it regularly to remind yourself of your true identity.

As you start to read the Bible more, you will see more and more of whose you are and who you are. That truth will set you free to love the real you and experience God's best.

> *To the Jews who had believed him, Jesus said, "If you hold to my teaching, you are really my disciples. Then you will know the truth, and the truth will set you free."*
>
> JOHN 8:31–32

▪ ▪ ▪

Source of Insight: The Spirit

Before the day of Pentecost, not all people who followed God had the ability to speak directly to Him. Instead, God only spoke directly to certain priests and leaders. Everyone else had to communicate with God through these specific people.

Now everyone in Christ has the ability to directly communicate with God (see Eph. 3:12). This is exciting but can also be confusing, especially if you're not familiar with this concept. Here are a few ideas that can help you in the process.

Free Up the Time: If you're someone who already knows how to talk with God and hear His voice, I encourage you to focus on clearing some intentional time in your schedule to speak with Him about your true identity. It may look like doing a prayer time. It could look like spending extra time at a worship service. It may entail going on a hike. It may mean not talking on the phone or listening to music during your commute. Or it could involve journaling or some other activity that helps you create space to hear God's voice. He's always speaking, but sometimes you just need to tune your spiritual radio channels to the right signal.

Once you create space, pay attention to what God says. Instead of talking the whole time, be open to listening.

Begin the Dialogue: If you're not as familiar with the idea of talking with God, no worries. There's no time like the present to start opening up greater lines of communication. I encourage you to think about it like you would cultivating a relationship with a new friend. As you spend more time with the person, you know him or her more and the flow of conversation becomes easier. The same is true with God.

One of the simplest ways you can start the conversation, especially in regard to understanding more of your true identity, is to ask God to give you wisdom.

In James 1, God says that He will give wisdom to you generously when you make the request with faith. Then, once you've asked, look for signs of God's voice everywhere. It may be in a verse of the Bible popping into your head for you to look up. It may be in a line an actor speaks in a movie sticking out to you. It may be a billboard. Or it may be a thought that comes into your head. If you're not sure if what you've heard is from God, see if it lines up with Scripture.

So if you hear something like "you're a horrible person who can never be forgiven," since that doesn't line up with all of the Scriptures that say you're redeemed, chosen, and forgiven, you can know it's not God. ("If we confess our sins, he is faithful and just and will forgive us our sins and purify us from all unrighteousness" [1 John 1:9].)

Pay Attention to Peace: If what you think you heard from God about your true identity lines up with Scripture, then test to see if what you heard gives you peace. I find that even when I hear hard things from God that the result of believing and following what He says is peace because I'm operating in alignment with His will.

If you don't feel peace about what you believe God told you about your true identity, ask Him for confirmation or consider going to some people who you trust to see what they sense from the Lord. It's good to hear from God and also to test the words to make sure that what you believe you've heard is accurate.

Be open to what God says about your true identity and then start living out of it. So if He tells you that He made you an artist, start trying out creative activities. You don't need to quit your job and open up a pottery studio. But you can and should start investing time in actions aligned with your artistic bent. If God tells you that you are not something, such as not gifted in administration, and you've been struggling in your volunteer service to coordinate activities, it may be time to resign. God didn't make us all to have the same identity, which means that He didn't give us all the same gifts and talents. You may have to do some required administration for your own life or work, but volunteering to do something misaligned with your gifts is often a poor choice. By being the true you and doing what He made you to do, you can enter into His best.

Don't fight what God tells you, embrace it. This in turn gives you the ability to love your true self and receive God's best.

■　■　■

Source of Insight: The Body

At its best, the body of Christ is a strong source of encouragement and accurately reflects the truth of who we are to us.

> *Therefore encourage one another and build each other up, just as in fact you are doing.*
>
> 1 THESSALONIANS 5:11

I know that this is unfortunately not always the case. I feel very sad when I hear of people quitting church and even abandoning their faith because of a bad experience with the people they encountered in a religious setting.

But it is still true that there are many good people who know and hear God who can help accurately reflect the truth of your identity to you. In my experience, this seems to work best when you simply remain open and allow God to move.

I've had dear friends whom I have known for years speak to me in a profound way about my particular identity in Christ. And I've had people whom I've only met once do the same in a powerful way. It's not so much about the people being perfect or about how long they've known you. Instead it's about God—who knows and loves you perfectly—speaking through them.

For example, I had a dear friend whom I have known for over seven years tell me that she saw me as a "beautiful, tender warrior." Then I had someone whom I spoke to for the first time when she was deciding to be part of my Divine Time Management group coaching program tell me, "You're powerful with a gentle touch."

Neither one of these were solicited comments. They simply arose spontaneously in conversation. I don't think I would have ever thought to describe myself in these ways. But both phrases struck me deeply as "true," and I immediately wrote them down. These words help remind me of my true identity, specifically how God tends to work through me. It makes me at peace with the fact that I may not come across as forcefully as others. But I'm doing exactly what I'm called to do as "me."

You may interact with people who say things like this to you spontaneously without you needing to ask for any insight. Or you may find it helpful to be a bit more explicit. For instance, it's a common assignment in university leadership classes for students to ask a variety of people who they know to describe a time when they saw them operating in their strengths. These stories from others of what they observed about their best selves can help them to understand who they are.

If you feel like God may want you to do this kind of exercise, then pray about whom to ask and what to ask them. Others can offer incredible perspective, but not everyone will clearly see your true identity. You want to be sure that you're talking with people who have accurate insight and will not put their own agendas ahead of your true self.

Again, if you're in doubt about what someone says about your identity, test it with Scripture, ask others, and then try it on for size. If it seems to fit you and feels comfortable and peaceful, it's probably from God. If it feels confining and gives you anxiety, it's probably not.

The identity God has given you leads to freedom, life, and should make everything feel in alignment. This puts you in the space of receiving God's best.

Source of Insight: The Anointing

Many parts of your true identity are ongoing. For example, I will always be a child of God. And I expect that in some form or another, I will always be a beautiful, tender warrior.

However, in certain times and seasons you can have specific

activities that God has given you to do in your time. Some people say this is a "calling," and others may use the terms an "anointing" or a "grace." Although these most definitely are part of who you are for a season, it's important that you don't see them as something that must always be part of your life for you to be OK. Otherwise something like being a pastor, worship leader, manager, soccer coach, or any other role can turn into a false identity that you insist on wearing instead of an anointing that you abide in as part of your true identity for as long as God gives it to you.

I really appreciated it when I heard a pastor once say that your one dream should be loving God and feeling His love in return, and you should look at everything else as just an assignment.

With that sort of perspective, you can then freely receive God's anointing for each season of your life. Let it rest in your hands with open palms so that when it's no longer your calling, God can easily pluck it away without the two of you getting into a fight.

So how do you know your anointing and abide in it?

Well, in the Scripture, anointing is something that God initiates. Sometimes it's through someone coming to people and telling them what they're called to do. For example, in 1 Samuel 16, the prophet Samuel goes to David's home and anoints his head with oil to be the next king. In other instances, God stirs up something internally within a person to do what He has called them to do. For example, Exodus 35:20–35 in the NASB version of the Bible talks about people's hearts stirring within them and their spirits moving them to contribute to the work of the tent of meeting as well as do craftsmanship like spinning fine linen, making engravings, and weaving.

I've seen God work in my life in both ways. For example, in one of my previous churches, I was asked to help with leading worship. I love worship music and try to have it on as much as possible. I'm one of the people you'll see singing loudly and raising my hands in church. But I quite honestly had never considered being a worship leader.

After someone asked me and I prayed about it, I realized I did have the desire to serve in that capacity. I needed to grow into the role, of course. But in the process of volunteering in leading worship, I experienced a great deal of joy, and others told me that they were blessed by my service. I left that church, and I don't know if I'll have future opportunities to serve as a worship leader. But the anointing was there for that season, and I'm grateful I could have that experience and be a blessing in that particular way.

I've also seen God give me an anointing by putting something deep in my heart that feels like part desire and part command. This book you're reading now is one of those times. I began to have a strong desire from God to write my first Christian book in September 2015. This was a big shift for me because I had published two other books, but they were both squarely in the business time management space. In many ways it didn't "make sense" from a practical point of view to make this shift into the faith realm. But I was so excited about the idea, and in my heart it felt "right." I couldn't start on the book proposal for this book until January 2016 because of some previous professional commitments. But I was just champing at the bit by then to get started. I considered it a joy to commit the time to writing a book proposal for *Divine Time Management*. And I was so incredibly grateful that proposal led to a contract and then to this book you're reading now.

No one told me that I had to write a book on a God-centered approach to time management. But the spirit inside of me made it clear that was the right move. Once this book is done, I trust God will be very clear on what's next.

Understanding what's your anointing for this season and what's not is really essential for living out your true identity and for investing your time in God's best.

So how do you get this clarity? As always, God can be creative, so these are not the only ways that He can speak to you, but as general guidelines, these three approaches can help.

Get Clear on What's Not Anointed: You may be doing some things or many things right now that were never your anointing or simply aren't your anointing anymore. Stop and evaluate with God where you feel frustrated and experience a lack of peace. Ask God why you're experiencing these struggles. If He tells you it's because you're not supposed to be doing one or more things, work with God on a transition plan. This realization can especially be hard when God calls you out of a ministry that you were very passionate about and thought would be a lifelong vocation. But when God tells you your time is done, obedience is the best option. He will provide for you and show you how your identity is secure even when you're not in the role that defined a big part of your identity in the past.

See What People Ask You to Do: Similar to me being asked to be a worship leader seemingly out of the blue, there may be times where inside or outside of the church people see gifts and talents in you that you didn't see in yourself. Pay attention to where you're asked to volunteer or step into leadership and prayerfully consider the opportunities. Maybe you never thought you would like working with children, but you have a special gift for it. Or maybe you didn't think you would be good at leading a special operations team at work, but God has set you up to excel in that area. As a word of warning, do not assume that because you're asked you are always supposed to say yes. Always stop and discern whether something feels right and that you have the time capacity to get it done. You don't want to get so overwhelmed with life, work, and service that you lose your connection with God and with your true self. Remember that everything you do should come from identity not be done for identity.

Pay Attention to Inner Stirrings: I find that when you're really meant to do something and God has given you an anointing, you almost can't help yourself from moving forward. You come up with great ideas without even trying, you have a surprising lack of fear of failure, and you're able to have an incredible amount of energy, even for really hard things. When something like this comes up inside of you, try to make space for it to grow. That could mean stopping with some existing responsibilities so you can pursue this new idea, whether it's a book, a special project, a service opportunity, or something entirely different. Then see what happens. I find that if it's just my idea, my enthusiasm tends to fizzle pretty quickly. But if it's God, I'm able to follow through, blessings come as I move forward in obedience, and the endeavor feels congruent with my true self.

As you become more and more aware of the anointing on your life at any particular time, you can live out the fullness of your true identity. When you're living out the fullness of your true identity, living a life in alignment with God and receiving His best then becomes possible.

Reflection Exercise: **LOVING THE TRUE YOU**

It can feel vulnerable to ask God to show you who you truly are, especially if you have strong views about who you believe you should be. These could be biases that came from media, that were imprinted on you by your family, that you acquired from friends, or that you simply picked up on your own.

As you uncover more and more of your true self, ask God to show you how who you truly are is special, wonderful, and enough.

I encourage you to not judge how God made you. For example, there are wonderful strengths from being good at planning and there are wonderful strengths from being naturally spontaneous. Both are valuable qualities within the right context. Neither is good or bad.

Most people will fall somewhere in the center when it comes to the spectrum of most character traits. Know your true self, accept your true self, and love your true self. In this process of becoming less judgmental of yourself, you will also have the added benefit of becoming less critical of others and allowing them to be their true selves.

God's best,
Elizabeth

For you created my inmost being;
you knit me together in my mother's womb.
I praise you because I am fearfully and wonderfully made;
your works are wonderful,
I know that full well.

PSALM 139:13–14

- - -

ALIGNMENT WITH GOD

CHAPTER 6

Right Relationship with God

Jesus replied: " 'Love the Lord your God with all your heart and with all your soul and with all your mind.' This is the first and greatest commandment."

MATTHEW 22:37–38

It's always interesting to notice how people who aren't Christians will comment on me being a "very religious" person when they hear me talk about what God is doing in my life. People who are Christians will usually say something like, "You're really on fire for the Lord."

I prefer the latter.

I don't primarily think of being a Christian as being a religion. I view it as an organic, dynamic, pulsating, living relationship. One based on fierce love, deep respect, and total commitment.

God's love for me will never waver, but the quality and depth of our relationship can vary dramatically based on my actions. If I choose not to grow our love or protect our love, it will wither and produce little fruit, just like in human relationships. But if I choose to abide in the vine, my life will prosper.

I want my heart's desire to be the same as the psalmist in Psalm 27:4:

One thing have I desired of the Lord, that will I seek
after; that I may dwell in the house of the Lord all the
days of my life, to behold the beauty of the Lord, and to
inquire in his temple.

(KJV)

RELATIONSHIP AND RULES

We covered discovering and loving your true identity first.
Because if you have a right view of who and whose you are,
you'll automatically have clarity on most of what you need to do
on a day-to-day basis.

When you're acting like your true self, you'll understand
what is and isn't right for you and how to do what you're doing
most of the time.

But some of your time management still might not be immediately clear. To gain total clarity of who you are and what you
should be doing involves the active, vibrant work of staying in
alignment. Since God's primary concern is relationship, alignment looks like having a right relationship with Him, with others, and with ourselves. That's what we'll cover in the three
chapters of this section.

God's a good dad and gives us clear general guidelines, hence
the gift of the Bible. But He doesn't want to simply hand us a
guidebook for life, punish us if we break the rules, and see us at
the end when we get to heaven and are perfect. God has a deep
desire to be on the journey with us, and that's why He'll give
us plenty of situations that don't fit a mold so that we'll need to
come to Him for direction.

God's ideal is that we live life like a partner dance where He's the lead, and we're the follow. We know the basic step, but we have to completely and consistently attune ourselves to Him in order to know when to twist, turn, dip, and spin. Since God can see everything all at once and deeply loves and cares for us, if we follow His lead—even when it doesn't make sense—we will enter into all of the good that He has for us.

ENTERING INTO RELATIONSHIP WITH GOD

To stay in relationship with God, you first need to *be* in relationship with Him. The Bible tells us that is possible by accepting Jesus Christ as your Savior.

> If you declare with your mouth, "Jesus is Lord," and believe in your heart that God raised him from the dead, you will be saved. For it is with your heart that you believe and are justified, and it is with your mouth that you profess your faith and are saved.
>
> (Romans 10:9–10)

> For God so loved the world, that he gave his only begotten Son, that whosoever believeth in him should not perish, but have everlasting life.
>
> (John 3:16 KJV)

> Jesus answered, "I am the way and the truth and the life. No one comes to the Father except through me."
>
> (John 14:6)

If you've never accepted Jesus Christ as your Savior, you can do so now by saying this prayer to God:

God, You say in Romans 10:9 that if we confess Jesus is Lord
and believe in our hearts that God raised Jesus from the
dead, we will be saved. Right now I confess Jesus as my Lord.
With my heart, I believe that God raised Jesus from the dead.
Right now, I accept Jesus Christ as my own personal Savior
and according to His Word, right now I am saved.
Thank You, God, for the grace and mercy available through
Jesus' life, death, and resurrection, which has saved me
from my sins. I thank You, God, that this grace leads me
to repentance. Therefore, God, transform my life so that I
may become more and more the image and likeness of Christ
Jesus and be in alignment with You and Your perfect will for
my life.

Whooo-hooo!!! Whether you just became a Christian in the last moment or have been one for all of your life, you're in for a wild and wonderful ride.

God is the most amazing father in the whole wide world. He has so much love to give you and so deeply desires to receive your love in return.

If you know intellectually that God is safe but are struggling emotionally with having the desire or ability to trust God, circle back to the section in chapter 2 on "Investing in Your Relationship with God." Go through the "Trust-Building Steps" until your heart is in a place of peace and you have the security to move forward without feeling afraid.

God loves you tenderly and wants to know you more. But

He will never force Himself on you or make you go faster in your relationship than feels comfortable to you. Please know that He will be gentle with your heart—especially if you've been wounded—and wants to be patient and kind with you.

STAYING IN COMMUNION WITH GOD

Once you've established a relationship with God, then it's time to develop it. Through developing that relationship, you will come to know God and hear His voice more clearly and easily on a moment-by-moment basis. And when you listen and obey, you will be in alignment and therefore investing your time in the best possible manner.

Developing your relationship with God requires both growing and protecting the love between the two of you.

Growing love includes the normal spiritual practices that most people think about, such as going to church, worshipping the Lord through music, spending time in the Word, and praying.

But God tells us that an essential part of growing love is also keeping His commandments (see John 14:15). That means that our obedience to what God speaks to us through His Word is as important as doing other religious activities. God loves us and wants the best for us, so doing what He says to do will not only make Him feel loved but also will always lead to the best outcomes in our lives.

In addition to growing love, we need to consciously protect the love in our relationship with God. The devil's desire is to separate us from God and others. To stay close, we need to engage in active resistance.

> Submit yourselves, then, to God. Resist the devil, and he
> will flee from you.
>
> (James 4:7)

One of the primary ways that the devil creates that separation is through tempting us to sin. That sin then creates distance between us and God.

> Surely the arm of the LORD is not too short to save, nor his
> ear too dull to hear.
> But your iniquities have separated you from your God;
> your sins have hidden his face from you, so that he will
> not hear.
>
> (Isaiah 59:1–2)

The way that we remove that block between God and ourselves is through acknowledging sin, being aware of negative influences, and forgiving.

I used to think that things like confessing sin were a one-and-done deal. Accept Jesus and you're good. But as I've learned more of the truth of God's Word, I've discovered that protecting my relationship with God is a daily, ongoing process, just like with people. Our awareness of what we need to do to remove barriers between God and ourselves is essential for staying in alignment with God through right relationship with Him.

So we'll start with a focus on growing love so we can have a solid relationship and then talk through protecting love so we can keep the love and alignment with God strong.

■ ■ ■

GROWING LOVE

Growing Love: No gods before God

> And God spoke all these words: "I am the LORD your God, who
> brought you out of Egypt, out of the land of slavery.
> "You shall have no other gods before me.
> "You shall not make for yourself an image in the form of anything
> in heaven above or on the earth beneath or in the waters below.
> You shall not bow down to them or worship them; for I, the LORD
> your God, am a jealous God, punishing the children for the sin of
> the parents to the third and fourth generation of those who hate
> me, but showing love to a thousand generations of those who love
> me and keep my commandments."
>
> EXODUS 20:1–6

Most of us live in cultures where there aren't ninety-foot-high gold statues that we're asked to bow down to like Shadrach, Meshach, and Abednego (see Dan. 3). But on a perpetual basis, we're tempted to commit idolatry by putting other gods ahead of the one true God. When we do that, we're out of alignment with God's best for us.

That could look like deciding that what we want to do is more important than what God wants us to do—idolatry of self and our will. That could look like centering our lives around other people and making all of our decisions around them first and then fitting in God around the edges—idolatry of people and relationships. It could look like putting achievement ahead of all other goals— idolatry of success or power. It could look like being primarily concerned with exercise and eating—idolatry of the body and health.

★ ★ ★

None of the above things are inherently bad, but when they come ahead of God, more or less saying to God, "No, I won't pay attention to what you want first because these other things come ahead of you," it's idolatry.

This is an area where I constantly need to be vigilant because for a long time, I didn't even realize that I had idols ahead of God. I thought it was "just normal" to make work or relationships my primary focus. But now I'm at least aware, and I've found centering my life on God has led to much better results with much less effort. For example, more contracts and opportunities have come in for my business—without me applying any more effort—when I was obedient to put working on this book for God ahead of business development.

To undergo this shift of heart, I encourage you when you make your goals for the year (if God even tells you to do this), plan your month, lay out your week, or write up your to-do list for the day, that your primary question is:

God, what do you want me to do?

Then listen. And do whatever He says.

Sometimes it might be very similar to what you would have planned. Other times, it might be very different. But if you're doing what God wants you to do, everything else is going to work out.

Looking to God, listening to Him, and doing what He says will deeply grow your love because God will feel so honored and you will feel so blessed. Expect that things in your life will work out miraculously down to the second when you practice this type of alignment with Him first. This is how you enter into God's best.

Growing Love: Worship

To be in alignment with God, we need to understand how great He truly is and put God in the right place in our minds, hearts, and spirits.

For example, let's say that you got assigned a new boss within your organization. He looked pretty ordinary, so you assumed he was probably just another mid-level manager without a whole lot of power or influence. You understood that he deserved some basic respect as your supervisor, but you weren't enamored of him.

Then, a few days later, a colleague asks you, "Hey! What do you think about the fact that you get to report to the new president and CEO?"

You do a double take. "What do you mean?"

He replies, "Didn't you realize that you're now reporting directly to the newly appointed head of our entire global organization?"

All of a sudden everything changes. You stand up a little straighter. Walk a little more confidently. Pick up within seconds when your boss calls because you realize you're working directly for the "big guy." Not only someone who can hire or fire you but who also has the ability to give you as much head count as you want, move billions of dollars with a single command, and get you tickets to all the major-league sporting events—including the playoffs. (Let's be honest, courtside seats are important.)

That's how worship moves in your heart to allow you to recognize how awesome and worthy of reverence God is. When you worship God, the love between the two of you flourishes, and a whole lot of issues that you spent a whole lot of time worrying about no longer seem significant.

You're aware of God's sovereignty and power, and doing what He says becomes a whole lot easier.

★ ★ ★

So how do you cultivate a lifestyle of worship?

One of the most obvious ways is through music—in the Bible we're told to sing praises to the Lord. That's why the song portion of church is often called the "worship" time. When I'm in those settings, I love to close my eyes, lift up my hands, and just imagine that I'm becoming one with everyone around me as we worship the Lord with one voice and one heart. It literally feels like a taste of heaven to me. I remember how big God is, how powerful He is, and how much He loves me.

I also find that playing worship music as much as possible throughout the week helps me to feel close to God and cultivate an attitude of faith and awe. In particular, worship music that focuses on how amazing God is helps me gain the right perspective that I can have total faith and confidence in God.

But the Word also talks about worship as a posture of surrender. Romans 12:1–2 reads:

> Therefore, I urge you, brothers and sisters, in view of
> God's mercy, to offer your bodies as a living sacrifice,
> holy and pleasing to God—this is your true and proper
> worship. Do not conform to the pattern of this world, but
> be transformed by the renewing of your mind. Then you
> will be able to test and approve what God's will is—his
> good, pleasing and perfect will.

So worship is not only a remembering of who God is but also a total giving of yourself to Him. In that complete gift of yourself, you are coming into alignment with God's will for your life and growing the love between you.

He will reveal what is right and good for you to do when

you're in the posture of worship. Sometimes that looks like Him talking to you during times of singing—I often end up pulling out my journal to write something down that He says. Other times it looks like you experiencing a deep peace when you finally let go of whatever you thought should be going on in your life and surrender to God's plans for you.

Worship changes our spiritual DNA and puts us in position for God to work in and through our lives to bring about His best.

※   ※   ※

Growing Love: Word

The Bible is God's love story to us.

It shows us how from the beginning, God desired us. He chose to create us. He wanted to love us. And even when we screw up again and again and again, He keeps forgiving us and taking us back again and again and again and again. He loved us so very much He gave His only begotten son to die for us— that's sacrifice to the highest degree.

When we read the Bible, we understand more of who God is and what He wants. This includes us having a more profound under-standing of God's greatness, like we get in worship. And it also shows us God's faithfulness, His love, His wisdom, His sovereignty, and so much more. The more we read the Bible, the more we desire God. The more we desire God, the more we align with Him.

Words of affirmation are something that touch my heart in a special way, so I also find that my love for God grows and my heart toward Him softens when I read these types of verses:

> "Therefore I am now going to allure her;
> I will lead her into the wilderness

and speak tenderly to her.
There I will give her back her vineyards,
and will make the Valley of Achor a door of hope.
There she will respond as in the days of her youth,
as in the day she came up out of Egypt.
"In that day," declares the LORD,
"you will call me 'my husband';
you will no longer call me 'my master.'
I will remove the names of the Baals from her lips;
no longer will their names be invoked.
In that day I will make a covenant for them
with the beasts of the field, the birds in the sky
and the creatures that move along the ground.
Bow and sword and battle
I will abolish from the land,
so that all may lie down in safety.
I will betroth you to me forever;
I will betroth you in righteousness and justice,
in love and compassion.
I will betroth you in faithfulness,
and you will acknowledge the LORD.
"In that day I will respond,"
declares the LORD—
"I will respond to the skies,
and they will respond to the earth;
and the earth will respond to the grain,
the new wine and the olive oil,
and they will respond to Jezreel.
I will plant her for myself in the land;
I will show my love to the one I called 'Not my loved one.'

I will say to those called 'Not my people,' 'You are my
people';
and they will say, 'You are my God.'"

(Hosea 2:14–23)

Reading God's Word puts us into a greater alignment with God because once we put Him first, by letting go of idols, and we recognize His awesomeness in worship, then our need to know His heart for us arises. Since the Bible reveals His steadfast heart of love toward us, we then realize that not only is God worthy of worship but also He's worthy of trust.

Once we know God is worthy of trust, then we can risk obeying what He says in His Word. When we obey what God says in His Word, we make God feel really loved and grow our relationship.

This is how we know that we love the children of God:
by loving God and carrying out his commands. In fact,
this is love for God: to keep his commands. And his commands are not burdensome.

(1 John 5:2–3)

"If you love me, keep my commands."

(John 14:15)

When you don't know what to do with a particular decision or how to use your time in general, turn to the Bible and seek truth there. In it you'll find a God who loves you, and timeless truths that pertain to all of life.

If you're not sure where to look, search online for a particular word related to the issue at hand, asking a question such as

"What does the Bible say about conflict?" Ask someone whom you trust for advice on what to read in the Bible that might help. Or simply pray and ask God to show you where to go in the Bible. The Word of God doesn't always tell us to do things that we want to do; it's not natural to desire to do things like bless those who curse us. But the Word does always lead to the most blessings for us and the most growth in our relationship with God when we follow it.

Growing Love: Prayer

Regular communication forms an essential part of any close relationship. That's why books like *The Seven Principles for Making Marriage Work* include "enhancing your love maps," i.e., being intimately familiar with each other's worlds, as principle number one.[17]

God never describes Himself as the distant rich uncle whom you turn to every few years when you're in a major crisis and need money, or the friend that you can go for years without talking to and then pick up your relationship as if no time has gone by.

Nope. God describes Himself as a loving, concerned, involved father when He relates to the church as His children. And He depicts Himself as a passionate, protective, devoted husband when He relates to the church as His bride.

In neither case does He want to be absentee or an acquaintance.

God deeply desires day-to-day communication with you. That is what most people would call prayer.

---

[17] John M. Gottman, PhD, and Nan Silver, *The Seven Principles for Making Marriage Work: A Practical Guide from the Country's Foremost Relationship Expert* (New York: Harmony, 2015), 53.

For all of the things that are on your heart, there are answers from God that He wants to give you. If those don't come through worship or the Word, they can come through prayer.

As I've described before, I intentionally set aside an extended time in the morning for reading the Bible, prayer, and journaling. But prayer is also simply part of my overall lifestyle. If I'm not talking on the phone when I'm on a walk or driving in my car, I'm praying. When I stop and take a lunch break, I'm talking life through with God. When I'm stumped about something, like what to write for a particular section of this book, I ask God what to do. When I'm feeling worried or anxious, I know it's time to turn to prayer. And when I'm SUPER happy, you better believe that I'm praising the Lord. Probably turning on some worship music and dancing around too! I think my neighbors find me peculiar, but I don't care.

Basically, I know that I'm never alone because God is my constant, faithful companion. Sometimes I'm asking God for things, but mostly I'm just living life with Him. And it's through that living life that the love in our relationship deepens and strengthens, I hear His voice, and I know His ways.

It's because of prayer that I live where I live. It's because of prayer that I knew to write this book. It's because of prayer that I have great peace, love, and joy in my relationships. And it's because of prayer that my body is healthy.

Ultimately, prayer is what calibrates me to God's heart and keeps me in step with His will and His ways. If I want to know how to use my time and what to do or not to do, communication with God through prayer provides the answer.

Prayer turns God from "God" to "my God," who is closer than my every breath and allows me to experience His best.

My prayer for you is that you will open yourself up to more time in prayer to grow your relationship with God and stay aligned with Him. There's not a right or wrong way to pray. Just say something or think something—anything—and then take it from there.

■ ■ ■

PROTECTING LOVE

As with most relationships, in our relationship with God, the best defense is a good offense. Spending time on growing love using all of the strategies described in the first half of this chapter will take care of at least 80 percent of being in right relationship with God—if not more. Growing love is your surest way to alignment.

When you love God, you want to do right by Him and you have a greater desire to obey.

How can a young person stay on the path of purity?
By living according to your word.
I seek you with all my heart;
do not let me stray from your commands.
I have hidden your word in my heart
that I might not sin against you.
PSALM 119:9-11

But even with the best of relationships, we sometimes get off track. That's natural and normal. It's not an issue to make mistakes. We're human and missteps happen to everyone. The important thing is that we recognize when we falter and make it right as soon as possible. In the following sections, we'll talk through ways in which you can protect the love between you and God so you stay in right relationship.

Protecting Love: Acknowledge Sin

We sin when we aren't in alignment with God's will. That could happen because we go against one of God's general commandments, like don't judge. Or that could occur when we do something that goes against our conscience in a particular situation, e.g., we know we shouldn't talk to a particular person about something, but we do anyway. This happens to all of us, so it doesn't need to be a source of shame but can be an opportunity for gratitude for the gift of forgiveness in Jesus Christ.

> If we claim to be without sin, we deceive ourselves and the truth is not in us. If we confess our sins, he is faithful and just and will forgive us our sins and purify us from all unrighteousness. If we claim we have not sinned, we make him out to be a liar and his word is not in us.
>
> (1 John 1:8–10)

In chapter 1, we went through different areas where we could ask forgiveness and return to God, specifically in regard to wrong goals for time management. Here I just want to encourage you that when you know you're doing anything that does not make God happy, you consider confessing—or admitting—your sin and then repenting, or turning from what you were doing to what God wants you to do.

As Christians, we're forgiven in Christ and adopted as God's children at the point of salvation. I believe we're a permanent member of the family. But we still need to say we're sorry and ask for forgiveness when we mess up to stay close to God, just like in a relationship with another person. You may love a person completely unconditionally. You can forgive him for anything. But the quality of your relationship with that person will be greatly enhanced if he confesses that he's done something wrong against you and then asks your forgiveness. The same is true with God.

Even though I've been a Christian my whole life, I really didn't understand the importance of repentance until about 2014. I figured that I was all set since I had confessed Jesus as my Savior (see Rom. 10:9). But as I studied the Word more and was around people who emphasized the importance of repentance, I realized how critical it was in a way that I never had before.

I now try to ask God's forgiveness immediately if something comes up for me. Usually I'll say something simple like "God, I repent for pushing ahead on what I wanted instead of asking you what you wanted" or "God, I ask your forgiveness for getting annoyed with the wait when I called the customer service line." By confessing our sin regularly, we stay intimate with God, can hear His voice, and remain in alignment with Him.

Repentance can also be done in prayer sessions with other people, particularly when you're trying to get breakthrough in an area such as not hearing God, struggles in a relationship, or even illness or addiction. When we ask God's forgiveness for sin, we free ourselves from the weight of the guilt of that sin and open up the door to a deeper and more intimate relationship with God.

Here's how King David described why it's important to acknowledge our sin:

When I kept silent,
my bones wasted away
through my groaning all day long.

> For day and night
> your hand was heavy on me;
> my strength was sapped
> as in the heat of summer
> Then I acknowledged my sin to you
> and did not cover up my iniquity.
> I said, "I will confess
> my transgressions to the LORD."
> And you forgave
> the guilt of my sin.
>
> (Psalm 32:3–5)

Here are some initial steps to take to acknowledge sin:

- Think of any current areas where you know that you have done something or are doing something that is not in alignment with God's will.
- Say, "I confess [the sin that you committed]. I'm sorry for committing this sin. And based on the finished work of Jesus on the cross, I accept your full forgiveness in Jesus' name. Amen."
- Repeat as often as necessary.

If you're prone to being very hard on yourself, remember that God loves you already right here, right now, just as you are. You don't need to spend all your prayer time apologizing for everything you've done or might have done. Just as things come up, acknowledge them, ask forgiveness, and move on in the freedom that is yours as a dearly loved and totally accepted child of God.

Protecting Love: Be Aware of Negative Influences

As someone who has worked in the self-help sphere for many years, I've become aware that negative influences don't always seem "negative" on the surface. There are many seemingly helpful sources of insight not aligned with God that come in very pretty packages. But just because something looks good doesn't mean that it is good. Remember the forbidden fruit? Yeah, that didn't go too well for humankind.

I encourage you in your journey to ask God for discernment about what you should or shouldn't do and whom you should or shouldn't listen to in terms of advice and insight. This matters, because what and whom you allow to influence your thinking and beliefs can have a dramatic impact on your relationship with God.

Some of the activities that may be having a negative influence on you are ones in which there is an emphasis on worship of things of this world, like money, fame, success, relationships, pleasure, or even the worship of self.

Having good things in your life is not a problem, and a healthy self-esteem is not a problem. But our primary aim should never be getting what we want out of life and promoting ourselves. And our source of power should always be God, not ourselves or worldly strategies. It's fine to learn and grow. But if our trust is in programs that promise to solve all our problems, we're putting them ahead of God.

I used to think that almost any advice that helped me get what I wanted was good to listen to and even try to implement. But I've come to realize I need to be careful about who and what I allow to influence me. As Colossians 2:8 says, "See to it that no one takes you captive through hollow and deceptive philosophy, which depends on human tradition and the elemental spiritual forces of this world rather than on Christ."

Now when I listen to or read information, I ask God to reveal His truth to me and highlight what is good and reveal what is not of Him. There are times when God has spoken to me in a profound way through someone or something that was not explicitly Christian but revealed His truth.

But at other times by listening to influences not of the Lord, I found that I had a tendency to chase after my worldly dreams instead of seeking God's will for my life. Or I simply ended up distracted by trying to make God's dreams for my life happen instead of trusting Him to fulfill His promises to me. I sometimes forget God doesn't need my help.

This striving to do what God has not called me to do is a tremendous waste of time and puts me completely out of alignment with Him. I find that when an "inspirational" message leads to fear, confusion, overwork, or pride, it's typically not of God. When it leads to peace, it is of Him.

Since I've become aware of the importance of paying attention to the positive or negative influence of advice, I've unsubscribed from a bunch of newsletter lists and stopped looking to certain experts. I find that I have fewer mentors to look to but that God has been faithful to lead and guide me in business and life. I'm flourishing more than ever both personally and professionally.

So if you've allowed influences in your life that pull you away from the Lord Jesus Christ instead of bringing you closer to Him, ask God for forgiveness for engaging in these activities in order to cancel the negative impact of them on your life. This could include non-Christian activities that had a negative impact on you. It could also include activities that were Christian on the surface but for whatever reason not led by the Holy Spirit.

Look to God for the answers you've been searching for elsewhere. Also, ask God to show you Christ-centered resources and people who can support you in your journey. When you're not swayed by negative influences, you will be able to hear God's voice clearly, know His will, and be clear on what to do and not do to align with the plans that He has for your time and your life.

　　■　　■　　■

Protecting Love: Forgive Others

We'll dive more into right relationship with others in the next chapter, but it is important to understand that to stay in right relationship with God, you need to stay in right relationship with other people. That means forgiving them when they've hurt or offended you.

> For if you forgive other people when they sin against you,
> your heavenly Father will also forgive you. But if you do
> not forgive others their sins, your Father will not forgive
> your sins.
>
> (Matthew 6:14–15)

Sometimes this will involve going to the other person, particularly if they know that they've hurt you. But many times it will mean that you forgive the person on your own in your private time with the Lord. If someone has deeply injured you, this may take a while. The forgiveness prayer is most effective when you not only forgive the person in general but also forgive the individual specifically for all of the hurt and negative consequences of his or her actions. If there have been many negative consequences, it can take time to uncover the layers. Sometimes you will forgive someone as best you know how at the time and then find even years later, that there are more levels of forgiveness that you need to go through.

When I'm going through this process, I find that it can be very helpful for me to write down all of the different ways in which I forgive the person and then burn the paper. The burning is a sign that I'm truly "letting it go" and not holding on to the offenses anymore.

To test whether you've forgiven the person, then try to bless her. If you can put yourself in the place of wanting the best for her, you know your heart is in a good place. Sometimes, I really can't do this right away. I need to come back another day or even another week. But I try to always get to the point of being able to bless so I'm following the command in Romans 12:14: "Bless those who persecute you; bless and do not curse."

When you're in a place of peace with those around you, you can be aligned with God in a loving relationship. When you're not, your judgment can be clouded, and you can be kept from experiencing unhindered closeness with God. This leads to lots of wasted time and energy because you're not connected to the vine. Forgiving others is as much about freeing yourself to experience God's goodness as it is about blessing them.

Congratulations! You've taken big steps forward in terms of being in alignment with God through growing and protecting love. That's the greatest commandment, so it's a wonderful start with being in alignment. But we can't stop there, so the next chapter covers how to stay in right relationship with other people.

Reflection Exercise: **HE NOTICES**

When I asked God what He wanted you to reflect on in regard to right relationship with Him, I felt He wanted me to tell you, "I notice." He notices when you spend time with Him, how much time you spend with Him, how much you share with Him, and how open your heart is.

He doesn't notice in the way that a strict teacher might: taking attendance and keeping track of participation points to grade you on how well you're performing.

He notices in a way a beloved friend or dear family member notices. He cares. When you make Him last priority or keep your heart guarded with Him, the distance between you hurts His heart.

In this coming week, focus on one habit you can integrate to grow love and consider whether there is anything you need to do to protect love to eliminate barriers in your relationship.

God's best,
Elizabeth

The LORD appeared to him from afar, saying,
"I have loved you with an everlasting love;
Therefore I have drawn you with lovingkindness."

JEREMIAH 31:3 NASB

CHAPTER 7

Right Relationship with Others

"And the second is like it: 'Love your neighbor as yourself.'"

MATTHEW 22:39

Control shows up in so many ways in relationships with others precisely because we can't control anyone. If we choose to accept that truth, we can experience deep peace. But if we don't, we become fearful. When we become fearful, we try to control our situations in a desperate attempt to make ourselves feel safe and secure.

Looking back over my life so far, I see where I've struggled and I see where I've grown. It's interesting to observe how different behaviors I just considered "normal" were actually not healthy. I hope in sharing some of my journey that God will reveal to you ways in which He wants to free you from control in relationships so you can experience God's best by finding your peace, safety, and security first and foremost in Him.

In my academic years, control in relationships came through being busy. Busy with classes, busy with studying, busy with extracurricular activities, busy with dance, busy with this and busy with that. I was a nice person so I had lots of people I knew whom I would talk to at school or activities. I had a few friends that I spent time with outside of scheduled activities, whom I still am grateful to have as friends to this day. But I didn't invest myself deeply and freely in those relationships because, well, I was busy.

★ ★ ★

My sense is that I'm not the only person who has done this. Sometimes there are legitimately busy seasons where you need to work or study more. But other times, being busy is an escape: a 100 percent foolproof way of being in control in your relationships. You simply reject everyone else before they reject you. No vulnerability. No risk. No mess.

If and when you decide to step out of the busy, you'll find that you have more time and more desire to have people in your life. That's what I found. When I got my life into better balance, all of a sudden my attention turned to people! Yeah!

But just because you start relating to people and really making time for them doesn't mean that you all of a sudden completely let go of control. What ended up happening—completely subconsciously—is that I decided to spread my relationship circle really, really wide instead of going deep. I was Miss Socialite. Out every night, on the phone constantly, and part of every young professional group in town. Literally.

This was a good step in the right direction, and I still have a few dear friends from this phase of my life. But once again, in time, God showed me that my approach to relationships was not truly based on trust in God. In my case, having a large array of friends was a form of self-protection. Subconsciously, I figured if I had a highly diversified relationship portfolio, I could avoid getting hurt. If a relationship dropped off, I had others to turn to because I wasn't overly invested in a particular person or group.

If you find yourself in this situation, where you know everyone but no one really knows you and you wonder if anyone really cares and will remember to do things like celebrate your birthday, it's time to take a step back. Evaluate. Ask God to show you what's really happening. There may be legitimate reasons for your behavior, such as business networking. But it's also possible that, like I was, you are avoiding emotional exposure and true vulnerability. If the latter is true, it's time to risk going deep.

God was so adamant that this change from wide to deep would happen in my life that He had me move from Iowa to Michigan to help with the process. It was a completely fresh start for me. In some ways it was exciting and in other ways terrifying. I went from a massive social circle to knowing next to no one. It felt to me like I was this giant flowering tree that had gotten pruned down to a measly stump—those kinds that look like sticks jutting from the ground.

With the intention of building deeper relationships and a sense of really belonging to a community, I began to develop my new life in Michigan. I knew fewer people but got to know them better. I also invested much more intentionally in some long-distance friendships. I chose not to be social every night and to select a few groups in which to deeply invest. I've been living this sort of lifestyle since 2009. I still enjoy networking events and adventures to mix life up, but in general, I'm content with a more grounded lifestyle.

This way of being is much more aligned with God's desire for my life. But even in this new and different way of being, I've found that God has had to break down mental models that can unintentionally put me into the control state. For example, I can have expectations about what a "friend," "family member," or "significant other" should do or be. But the truth is that each person is free to do or not do as they please. And each relationship is entirely different. And even within specific relationships, there is constant change and flux.

To be most healthy in relationships, I'm learning that we need to let go of rigid mental models of how our relationships "should be" and to accept them as they are, be ourselves, encourage others to be themselves, and freely give and receive. This ends up looking less like having a relationship organizational chart and more like being at a great big dance. During this dance, I have some primary dance partners, but then I have lots of other people whom I "dance" with throughout the day. With this mentality toward relationships, love and healing can flow freely.

I am a completely different person than I once was. My past does not define my present and future because God has healed me, is healing me, and will heal me. I truly believe there is nothing broken in me that God can't fix. I pray that you have the same hope in God for yourself, whatever relational challenges you may face. You can be freed and healed in Christ. And, just as you are right now, you are already completely loved and worthy of love.

God calls us to deeply invest in relationships and to focus on giving in trust that there is no hurt that He cannot heal and that He will supply all of our needs. When we let go of the fear of being hurt or not getting, we receive more than we could have ever dreamed possible. Brad Powell, senior pastor at NorthRidge Church, describes this sacrificially generous love as what shifts love from transactional worldly love to the transformational love of Christ.[18] This is where miracles occur, not only in our relationships but also in ourselves. We become one with Christ's suffering and witness the power of His resurrection. No control. No fear. No shame. Just love.

REAL CONNECTIONS WITH REAL PEOPLE

> The LORD God said, "It is not good for the man to be alone. I
> will make a helper suitable for him."
>
> GENESIS 2:18

---

[18] Brad Powell, "Love…Is Generous" (sermon at NorthRidge Church, Plymouth, Michigan, December 17, 2016), http://northridgechurch.com/experience/talks /loveis-generous/187.

Even before man had damaged his relationship with God through sin, God said that it wasn't good for him to be alone. People need other people. Jesus said it was the second greatest commandment to love others as ourselves. That means that it's not optional, it's essential.

In our fractured world, being open to relationships requires courage to be vulnerable and the risk to put others before ourselves. But these leaps of faith are possible when we entrust our heart and our healing to God.

When we open ourselves up to authentic, deep relationships, the payoff is enormous. So much of what we long for in terms of healing, a sense of belonging, and a feeling of joy and safety to fully and freely be ourselves can only happen in and through relationships. We cannot enter into God's best if we are not in right relationship with those around us.

As with staying in right relationship with God, staying in right relationship with people involves two parts: cultivating love and guarding your heart.

Some of the ways we can cultivate love include:

- By Giving
- By Peacemaking
- By Intentionality
- By Vulnerability

To keep these relationships healthy, we also need to guard our hearts God's way. This happens through these strategies:

- Pray More, Worry Less
- Point the Finger...At Yourself

- Be Wise as Serpents and Innocent as Doves
- Use the Jesus Shield

We'll cover all of these topics in this chapter. As you read, I hope you will keep this thought in mind. It's a quote from a commencement speech by Adrian Tan for the Nanyang Technological University in Singapore:

> I exhort you to love another human being. It may seem odd for me to tell you this. You may expect it to happen naturally, without deliberation. This is false. Modern society is anti-love. We've taken a microscope to everyone to bring out their flaws and shortcomings. It's far easier to find a reason not to love someone, than otherwise. Rejection requires only one reason. Love requires complete acceptance. It is hard work.... In loving someone, we become inspired to better ourselves in every way.... Loving is good for the soul.[19]

▪ ▪ ▪

CULTIVATING LOVE

Cultivating Love: By Giving

There's a time and place for setting boundaries—we'll talk about that more later in this chapter. But I believe that God desires the

---

[19] Adrian Tan, "Don't Work. Be Hated. Love Someone," available at: https://www.cs.uic.edu/~jjoseph/articles/DontWork.BeHated.LoveSomeone..pdf.

first inclination of our heart to be to give because that's the first inclination of His heart.

Especially in modern Western cultures, the first inclination of many people is to not give or be generous with our time or other resources. This is not true of all people, of course. I'm sure many people reading this book are extremely giving and may even need to rein themselves in a bit to stay aligned with God. But as a general society, we tend toward the way of independence and isolation.

I believe that one of the reasons this happens is due to the faulty impression we have that our time and our life are our own. The sense that we don't owe anyone anything—not even God—and that we're free to do whatever we want with what we have. This perspective not only makes it difficult for us to cultivate love but also it's simply not biblical:

> *"You have heard that it was said, 'Love your neighbor and hate your enemy.' But I tell you, love your enemies and pray for those who persecute you, that you may be children of your Father in heaven. He causes his sun to rise on the evil and the good, and sends rain on the righteous and the unrighteous. If you love those who love you, what reward will you get? Are not even the tax collectors doing that? And if you greet only your own people, what are you doing more than others? Do not even pagans do that? Be perfect, therefore, as your heavenly Father is perfect."*
> MATTHEW 5:43-48

> Do you not know that your bodies are temples of the Holy Spirit, who is in you, whom you have received from God? You are not your own; you were bought at a price.
>
> (1 Corinthians 6:19–20a)

> Therefore, I urge you, brothers and sisters, in view of
> God's mercy, to offer your bodies as a living sacrifice,
> holy and pleasing to God—this is your true and proper
> worship.
>
> (Romans 12:1)

As Christians, our lives aren't our own anymore. God tells us to be loving toward others, so when that encompasses also giving of our time, we need to be open to doing so.

And when we give of our time, which is the most valuable resource we have, we need to do so without fear of getting taken advantage of and without scorekeeping. A giving person doesn't do things simply based on reciprocity, i.e., you give to me and then I'll give to you and so on and so forth. A giving person just gives without expecting anything in return, knowing that if God is calling him to do the giving, he will be taken care of. Here's what Jesus says on the topic:

> Give to the one who asks you, and do not turn away from
> the one who wants to borrow from you.
>
> (Matthew 5:42)

I don't know about you, but hearing the radicalness of Jesus' commands makes me super nervous. One part of me wants to be free to be totally generous, and the other part of me can get afraid—what if there's not enough left for me?

In wrestling with this issue, I've seen that these principles can help us put Jesus' words into action and cultivate love by being giving, particularly with our time.

Let God Lead: We need God to show us how and when He wants us to be generous. Even Jesus did not do what everyone asked Him to do. He did the Father's will. If we are in God's will, all our needs will be taken care of. If we go outside of God's will, we can get in trouble with our giving because we're giving more than God is asking us to give.

As we go through life and feel an urge to give of our time, money, or other resources, we need to ask God to show us: Is this of God or is this of ourselves? I find that when it comes to growing in giving, one sign it's of God is that the thought or feeling that I should do a certain generous act persists over the course of days or weeks. If a thought is not of God, it tends to quickly come and go.

Also, another typical key sign that we are in God's will is a sense of peace. I find that when you're growing in giving of your time, money, or other resources, that the "peace indicator" is a little more nuanced than normal. Here's what I've seen: If it is God's will for you to grow in giving, you may not feel at peace about the act of giving. But you will be even more unpeaceful about the alternative of not going through with giving. Letting go of fear regarding generosity takes courage.

Here's an example to illustrate how the peace indicator can play out when it comes to giving, God's way: Let's say that you have a friend who you know is going through a really hard time. You told her that you would bring dinner over to her on a Tuesday night to cheer her up and to spend time with her. On that Tuesday, you get slammed at work, and you feel like you have far more to get done than you have time to get things done. You're feeling overwhelmed and consider canceling.

Instead of immediately canceling, you take time to pray about it and ask God to give you wisdom on whether you should stay and work late or keep your commitment to your friend. You still feel some anxiety about how everything will get done with work.

The numbers don't add up in terms of the time required to finish the tasks. But you have absolutely no peace about canceling with your friend. You get a very strong sense that it's important to keep that commitment. Although you don't feel peaceful on the surface about going to see your friend, deep down you have peace that it's the right choice—that it's in alignment with God.

If your experience ends up being anything like mine has been, you'll find that when you give your time in the way God wants you to give, He will absolutely take care of everything else working out. From canceling meetings to making work go faster to giving you favor with others to switch around deadlines or delegate work, God will provide for all of your needs when you do what He calls you to do in giving of your time.

Think Small: So often when we think of giving, we can think that it needs to be big, official, and fancy. But that's not the case. When we're cultivating a generosity of spirit, it's about the small, everyday choices. Maybe it looks like offering to take in a cart for a stranger who just finished unloading into her car as you're walking into the grocery store. Maybe it looks like taking a few moments to pray for a friend and sending a text to let him know that you're praying for him. Or maybe it looks like stopping to really listen to your child when she's trying to tell you something instead of half listening and half doing something else.

I find that being giving is about a lifestyle of engaging with opportunities to be generous in the moment. It's good and right to do this in an official capacity with volunteer organizations. But even more important, I believe God wants us to appreciate the everyday moments with the people around us.

When we're giving with our time, we are cultivating right

relationships with others and we can enter into the fullness of life that God has for us.

Cultivating Love: By Peacemaking

If it is possible, as far as it depends on you, live at peace with everyone.

ROMANS 12:18

Similar to how most Western societies tend to be anti-giving, they also tend to be anti-peacemaking. Think of it. The vast majority of news programming as well as most talk shows and sitcoms would get canceled if the emphasis were on peace instead of conflict.

It's easy to point a finger at our secular culture and say, "See! How awful."

But if we're honest, those within the body of Christ can be some of the worst at peacemaking. This can happen within churches, between church bodies, and between church people and the "outside" world. Offense, judgment, control, criticism, and all sorts of other things can absolutely run rampant. When it does, we poison ourselves and weaken the body of Christ.

Does that mean that we don't believe there is truth or say what is true? No. But it does mean that we try to be at peace with all men—and women—as Jesus commands us to do. This not only aligns us with God's will, but also shows the truth of who Christ is to the world. Plus it saves us so much time because being in conflict with others can drain our energy and hours more than almost anything else.

Here are two ways that we can cultivate love by peacemaking:

Avoid Being Offensive On Purpose: We can say what we believe to be true in a way that promotes unity or in a way that promotes division. I know that Jesus occasionally spoke in very harsh tones, but He was perfect. We're not. So I believe as people of faith, we need to try to be peacemakers and use soft words to turn away wrath.

> *A gentle answer turns away wrath,*
> *but a harsh word stirs up anger.*
> PROVERBS 15:1

As an example, let's take a very controversial subject such as abortion. I personally believe that God says in Psalm 139:13 that He knit me together in my mother's womb and that my life was real and mattered to Him even before I was born.

You may hold the same view as I do or you may not. But all of us can decide how and when to express our point of view. First of all, we need to use great wisdom to know whether or not to bring it up. In some situations, God is asking us to speak what we believe. In other cases, it's simply time to keep silent and pray and love. There are many reasons that people could be pro-life or pro-choice, and depending on the situation, speaking our point of view could cause more harm than help.

Second, if you do feel that God is telling you to speak up about something such as the issue of abortion, you have choices about how you communicate. If you're pro-life, one option could be to say something like: "I could never vote for that person because he promotes murdering babies." Although that may be what you believe to be true, that tone and style of communicating will create offense with someone who has a different point of view. Not only will that make it really hard for her to hear you when you explain your reasoning behind why you think the way you do but also you have a good chance of harming the relationship with the person in general. That means you're not living at peace with all people, and you're closing the opportunity for people to see Christ in you. That's not alignment with God and entering into God's best.

A different choice you have to speak the truth in love is to say something like, "I have a very high regard for human life. I think all of us can appreciate how heart-wrenching it is to see a little preemie baby in NICU. We all hope and pray for miracles and that that little vulnerable child will grow and develop into fullness of life. I feel that way about all children, including those who are currently unborn. That's why I choose to vote the way that I do."

In the second case, you're stating a clear opinion aligned with your understanding of the Bible, but you're doing it in a way that promotes peacemaking. There's a very high chance that you'll stay in right relationship with the other person, no matter what her views, because you're cultivating love instead of destroying it.

Could someone still get offended? It's probable. But the likelihood is much less. In cultivating peace, you're showing Christ and bringing God's best into the world.

Assume the Best: If we wanted to do just one thing to cultivate more peace in our lives and our relationships, assuming the best would be one of the most important activities for us to do. This is true in all relationships but especially true in our most sacred ones, such as marriage. Here's what four decades of scientific research on marriage has shown:

What can make a marriage work is surprisingly simple. . . . [Happily married couples] have hit upon a dynamic that keeps their negative thoughts and feelings about each other (which all couples have) from overwhelming their positive ones. Rather than creating a climate of disagreement and resistance, they embrace each other's needs. When addressing a partner's request, their motto tends to be a helpful "Yes, and..." rather than "Yes, but..." This positive attitude not only allows them to maintain but also to increase the sense of romance, play, fun, adventure, and learning together that are at the heart of any long-lasting love affair.[20]

So whether it's your significant other, friend, coworker, or the person driving next to you on the highway, we can cultivate love and make peace by choosing to assume the best. That means when someone doesn't call you or text you back, you assume that they maybe didn't get the message or saw it and were super busy in the moment. Instead of getting angry or hurt, you reach out again and say something like, "Not sure if you got my message, but I was wondering XYZ."

That means if someone cuts you off on the highway, you assume that they were being absentminded or didn't see you instead of thinking they were purposely trying to be obnoxious. That means if your spouse comes home late from work, you assume he was trying the best he knew how to get home on time. Or if your coworker says something aggressive in a meeting, you assume that she didn't mean to come across as disrespectful—she was just stressed.

Simply assuming the best and letting things go is one of the

---

[20] John M. Gottman, PhD, and Nan Silver, *The Seven Principles for Making Marriage Work* (New York: Harmony, 2015), 4–5.

most powerful tools we have to cultivate love and maintain the peace. In doing so, we enter into God's best and save an immense amount of time being frustrated and then having to deal with the fallout when those pent-up negative emotions explode.

■ ■ ■

Cultivating Love: By Intentionality

To cultivate deep, lasting, satisfying relationships with others, it takes intention. Sometimes that just means being open when the opportunity to connect comes, like saying yes when your colleagues ask you to go out to lunch with them or stopping to chat when you notice your neighbor out in his yard.

But often it also means being proactive to show that you care about another person and value staying connected with her.

You can't force a relationship. It's a gift. But when the potential for a relationship comes or is present, you can cultivate that seed and see what blossoms. Sometimes nothing comes of it. Certain people may not be open to a deeper relationship with you or simply may not have the time. But when you find a situation whether it's with family, friends, or others where there's a mutual desire for more connection, beautiful things can develop, and you can enter into God's best for your relationships.

Here are two key ways that you can be intentional in your relationships:

Create Systems for Thoughtfulness: As a time management coach, I'm a huge fan of using my calendar to help me remember all sorts of things, from paying quarterly taxes to setting up doctors' appointments.

Because investing in relationships is one of my top priorities, I also have calendar reminders for remembering to stay in touch.

Usually I remember without the calendar reminders, but having them in place ensures I'm intentional.

Here are examples of a few ways that I have systems for thoughtfulness:

- **Birthday Notices:** I put reminders in my calendar as annual recurring events for all key birthdays. If the person is someone to whom I would want to mail a card or gift, I also put in an annual reminder a few weeks before her birthday to shop for those items.
- **Regular Calls:** With my parents, brother, and sisters, I have a conference call on a weekly basis. My family has been doing weekly calls together for over sixteen years. We all call into a conference number and each have a chance to chat about our week. This is a way for us to all intentionally stay up to date on one another's day-to-day lives despite living in different parts of the country.
- **Recurring Reminders:** I have recurring monthly and quarterly reminders to make sure that I've set up times to meet in person with certain friends. Often by the time I see the reminder, I've already gotten get-togethers set up with most of them. But this notice in my calendar is a simple way for me to make sure that I don't unintentionally let important friendships wither because I simply forgot to be in touch.

I encourage you to think about whom God is telling you to be more intentional with in your life. It could be a friend or a colleague or your significant other or your mom or your child or someone entirely different. Then think about what simple systems you can put in place to be intentional about cultivating those relationships.

Speak the Right Love Languages: Love languages are the way in which you communicate care for another person. Gary Chapman's book for couples, *The 5 Love Languages: The Secret to Love That Lasts*, takes an in-depth look at this concept. As Gary outlines, these are the five primary love languages:

- Quality time
- Acts of service
- Physical touch
- Receiving gifts
- Words of affirmation[21]

Yet we can apply these not only to romantic love but to all different types of relationships. To get the most bang for your time and effort, being aware of and intentional about speaking other people's "love languages" can really help. It's important when we want to cultivate love in our relationships that we're aware of what makes the other person actually feel cared for and loved. Not everyone responds to the same gestures of kindness in the same way. Something that could mean nothing to you could be very important to someone else or vice versa. We'll cover a brief summary of what you need to know to be intentional.

Most people have a top two or three love languages that are very meaningful to them. This means that if you invest time

---

[21] Gary Chapman, *The 5 Love Languages: The Secret to Love That Lasts* (Chicago: Northfield Publishing, 2015).

in speaking those to them, it will make them feel very loved. If you don't, they will probably not feel loved by you even if you are very lavish in the other areas. So, for example, if you have someone whose primary love language is receiving gifts and you spend lots of time with her and lavish her with words of affirmation but don't give her gifts, she probably won't feel loved. The opposite is also true. If someone's top love language is quality time and you give him many things but don't spend time with him, he won't feel loved. Applying the concepts from Chapman's work can help you to maximize the impact of the time you invest in letting others know that you care about them. Using this knowledge can also minimize the time you need to spend fixing issues created by the people in your life feeling unloved.[22]

This level of intention will deepen and strengthen your rapport and lead to all the blessings God wants to give you in your relationships.

Cultivating Love: By Vulnerability

In *Daring Greatly: How the Courage to Be Vulnerable Transforms the Way We Live, Love, Parent, and Lead*, the author Brené Brown officially defines vulnerability as "uncertainty, risk, and emotional exposure"[23] but I like her unofficial description better: "Vulnerability sounds like truth and feels like courage."[24]

It can feel extremely risky to be and share the truth of who

---

[22] Ibid.

[23] Brené Brown, PhD, LMSW, *Daring Greatly: How the Courage to Be Vulnerable Transforms the Way We Live, Love, Parent, and Lead* (New York: Gotham Books, 2012), 34.

[24] Ibid., 37.

we are in our relationships. But it's the only way to freedom for ourselves and the only way to cultivate rich, deep, true relationships with others. As Brown shares later in *Daring Greatly*, "The irony is that when we're standing across from someone who is hiding or shielded by masks and armor, we feel frustrated and disconnected. That's the paradox here: *Vulnerability is the last thing I want you to see in me, but the first thing I look for in you.*"[25]

God, in creating humanity—you, me, everyone—saw that there was vulnerability and that it was good. God could have chosen to not have children. It's just easier with everyone and everything being perfect. No messes, no heartache, no betrayal, no evil, no uncertainty. But knowing all that we would do to Him and to His son Jesus and to each other and the anguish that would put them through, He still felt making us was worth it—totally worth it.

So to be in right relationship with others and align with God's heart, we have to choose the way of vulnerability.

I'm not saying to have no boundaries and dump everything on everyone all the time. But what I am saying is that with the people God has put in your life who are safe and worthy of trust, you will experience right relationship by showing up in an authentic, vulnerable way.

The book *The Big Leap: Conquer Your Hidden Fear and Take Life to the Next Level* explains vulnerability in relationships—particularly communication in relationships—in this way:

> Behind every communication problem is a sweaty ten-minute conversation you don't want to have. However, the

---

[25] Ibid., 113.

moment you work up the courage to have it, you collect an instant reward in relief as well as open up a flow of communication that will allow you to resolve the situation.[26]

And later in *The Big Leap*, there's this insight:

Under the surface of most conflicts, you'll find that the warring parties are actually feeling the same deeper emotions.... When they get beneath the roiled surface of the issue, they discover that the real issue is that they're both sad about something they've both kept hidden.... Once I see people communicating about the deeper feelings, I know that it's possible for the miracle of rebirth to occur in the relationship. Now they're communicating as allies, not as enemies, and when people do that, real-life miracles are possible.[27]

So when it comes to cultivating love, I would like you to reflect on your life and ask yourself if there are any areas with communication issues: Is there someone you're not speaking to right now? Someone who you should have a close, vulnerable connection with but whom you keep at a distance? Or even a person or people where you're in outright conflict?

Then ask God if it's time for you to communicate in an open, vulnerable way in these situations. At times, God will discourage you from reopening a relationship. It may not be healthy or appropriate for you to be in communication with certain people.

[26] Gay Hendricks, *The Big Leap: Conquer Your Hidden Fear and Take Life to the Next Level* (New York: HarperOne, 2009), 52.
[27] Ibid., 106–107.

But other times, God will ask you to try again. When you try again, choose the way of vulnerability instead of self-protection.

For example, that might sound like you saying: "I know we've been having some disagreements recently. I would like for us to have some time to reconnect and for me to really hear what you've been feeling and experiencing."

Then if the person is open to that conversation, do what you said and listen. Don't come in with a big monologue or rebuttals, just listen and affirm the other person's experience. After you've listened to him, if you're both open to it, share what's been on your heart. Not in terms of everything he's done wrong but simply in terms of what you've been feeling and experiencing.

You may not come to an agreement immediately. But you can start moving toward empathy and understanding for each other as human beings, and that opens up space for God to work to do the healing.

In choosing the way of vulnerability, we are truly choosing the way of love. In doing so, we enter into right relationship with others and experience all the good that God wants to bring forth in our lives.

■ ■ ■

GUARDING YOUR HEART

Focusing on cultivating love is the best way to ensure that you stay in right relationship with others. But even with a really good offensive game of cultivating love, you still need a defense. The devil is constantly on the prowl looking for ways to try to destroy you and your relationships and—I hate to break it to you—you're not perfect. So that's why, to stay in right relationship with others and therefore enter into God's best, you need to also guard your heart.

> Watch over your heart with all diligence,
> For from it flow the springs of life.
> PROVERBS 4:23 NASB

The first two areas in regard to guarding your heart involve asking God to pull the proverbial plank out of your own eye before you get too hung up on anything the other person did or didn't do. In those sections, we'll cover praying more so you worry less and pointing the finger... at yourself.

Then the second two areas do involve looking at the other person in the relationship and assessing with God's help what needs to be done. There are times when it is right and good to limit or even end a relationship. In these circumstances, we'll explore what it could mean to be wise as a serpent and innocent as a dove and how to set boundaries using something I call the "Jesus shield."

Most of all, we must pray and ask God for His protection. The devil hates connection, he hates relationship, he hates love, he hates vulnerability, and he wants to isolate you. But the Holy Spirit is greater than any evil forces, and no matter what the devil tries against you or those whom you love, you can prevail with the Lord's help.

Guarding Your Heart: Pray More, Worry Less

I think that worrying about our relationships—especially for women—may be one of the biggest ways in which we spend time in a way that is absolutely out of alignment with God's best for our lives. This does no good for our relationships with others and wastes so much of our life.

God tells us not to worry many times in the Bible with this verse being among the most popular:

> Do not be anxious about anything, but in every situation,
> by prayer and petition, with thanksgiving, present your
> requests to God. And the peace of God, which transcends
> all understanding, will guard your hearts and your minds
> in Christ Jesus.
>
> (Philippians 4:6–7)

And Jesus tells it like it is in Luke 12:22–26:

> Then Jesus said to his disciples: "Therefore I tell you, do
> not worry about your life, what you will eat; or about
> your body, what you will wear. For life is more than food,
> and the body more than clothes. Consider the ravens:
> They do not sow or reap, they have no storeroom or barn;
> yet God feeds them. And how much more valuable you
> are than birds! Who of you by worrying can add a single
> hour to your life? Since you cannot do this very little
> thing, why do you worry about the rest?"

So how do we know when we're worrying about our relationships, and how do we guard our hearts to get out of the worry place and into God's peace within ourselves and our relationships?

One of the first things to do is to recognize the difference between concern and worry. Concern tends to fall within the realm of addressing legitimate issues where your actions can have an impact. For example, telling your son that there's a snowstorm in your area so he should plan extra time when he drives home for Christmas. In contrast, worry is when you're thinking about potential what-if scenarios that you have no control over: they were never within your control or you've done everything that you could do, and now thinking about them further only creates anxiety. For example, after you've told your son about the snowstorm, worrying would look like feeling tense all day, texting him constantly to check in on him, and picturing him getting in bad accidents.

Concern profits. Worry destroys.

Instead of allowing our thoughts to loop again and again imagining the worst-case scenarios, we need to choose to pray and then give situations to God. Even in the case of concern, we need to take care to not go overboard. I'm naturally a planner so sometimes I can take concern a little too far, thinking through scenarios and even conversations in advance.

When I notice myself thinking again and again about a situation with another person, I know I'm not in a place of trust in God and probably not in right relationship with the other individual involved. Usually this repeated thinking about a situation—what I'm going to do or say—is a form of self-protection. It's a way to use worry to feel like I'm in control by mastering the situation in my mind. But the truth is that I'm never in control of other people and when I surrender to that truth in my heart, allow myself to feel the vulnerability of that truth, and surrender the situation to God, then I can experience God's peace.

Once I've done that, then I need to consciously tell myself

to start thinking about something different and to trust that I can show up without fear, be present with the person, and know everything will work out. Ultimately, I'm responsible for myself, and I can't and shouldn't try to control other people's responses to me. My prayers shouldn't be "God, please have this person do this or that"; instead, my prayers should be for God's will to be done and for me to say and do what God wants me to say and do.

Another way to guard your heart by praying more and worrying less is by staying out of situations that aren't yours to fix. As kids we used to say, "Mind your own business." That simple phrase was pretty accurate. So often you worry because you want to try to fix something completely outside of your control. As the oldest of four children and also as a coach, I have to be careful to not fall into this trap. It's common for me to think of what I believe would be a brilliant idea for someone else. Or I can see a potential issue that someone may have in the future and want to give her guidance to prevent it. But ultimately, if someone does not ask me for advice and I'm not in an official role like being a coach or someone's parent, it's not my place to offer suggestions on what to do. And it's absolutely not my place to feel responsible for others' actions. For young children under my care, I do have a responsibility for their health and safety. But for adults, you and I need to let go and trust God to take care of everything. When in doubt, pray for them and, to the best of your ability, stop thinking about it.

When you guard your heart from worry through prayer, you end up in alignment with God, right relationship with others, and free up so much time to think about productive things like what God is calling you to do at any particular moment.

Guarding Your Heart: Point the Finger...At Yourself

In terms of staying in right relationship with others and having your time aligned with God's best, letting go of worry will move you a big step forward. Once that's done, then it's time to look inward at your reactions to other people instead of immediately jumping to blame them for how you feel. This literally could save you years of being upset and fix the majority of your relationship issues.

> "Why do you look at the speck of sawdust in your brother's eye and pay no attention to the plank in your own eye?"
>
> MATTHEW 7:3

This step is a hard and humbling one to take. Personally, I sometimes don't like it. At times, it feels easier to jump to blaming someone else for how I feel hurt, afraid, upset, or insecure, than it is to look within myself to figure out what needs to heal.

However, I've found counterintuitively that when I take ownership of my response to someone else, I'm happier and most of all *free*. I'm no longer giving other people the ability to control how I feel or don't feel at any particular moment.

This is not an easy process, but with the Lord's help, it can be done. Here are some steps that I've found helpful:

Identify What Exactly Happened: When you're upset about what someone did or didn't do, it's really important to go beyond the surface-level assessment of the situation to figure out what really happened. Many times your reaction has to do with not just the exact moment but also the context around the moment as well as previous history. Ask yourself: *Was something else going on in my life that had an impact on how I saw this event? Had something happened previously in this relationship that colored how I saw this person? Am I tired, stressed, hungry, hot, or in any* *other way mentally, emotionally, or physically agitated?* Get data on all the different aspects of yourself and the situation before you start to draw conclusions.

Ask Why It Triggered You: Your reaction to a particular situation you have with a person has more to do with you than it has to do with them. When you have a negative reaction to someone, it typically stems from hurt, insecurity, fear, or something else broken inside of you. When that broken part of you is triggered, you can respond with strong negative emotions and also tell yourself bad stories that feed those emotions.

For example, let's say that a close friend doesn't call you back for a few days after you leave a message. If you feel secure in yourself and your relationship with your friend—you know that she loves and cares for you—you'll tend to assume the best and simply call her again without being upset. But let's say that you don't feel secure in yourself and in your relationship with a particular friend. Maybe you have struggled with developing friendships in the past and doubt your ability to be a good friend. Or maybe you have had repeated experiences with this friend not responding to your messages so there's a history of hurt. When she then doesn't respond to your message, you can get really angry about the situation. You can also tell yourself negative stories about her just ignoring you or being a bad person.

> *The wall around our hearts is constructed of bricks of fear and mortar of pride.*[28]
> —THERESA MILLER

Repent and Forgive: If you've allowed your mind to judge the other person, you'll need to repent for judgment (see

---

[28] Theresa Miller, prayer call, March 28, 2016.

Matt. 7:1–2). That could sound like, "I repent for judging [person] for [action that I found upsetting]."

The action someone else took may not be good. But as Christians, we're simply not allowed to judge, otherwise we can fall into judgment. (If we're honest, there's at least a time or two when we haven't returned a phone call or done something else perfectly.) We also need to ask forgiveness of God for any other sin that we've fallen into like bitterness, anger, jealousy, revenge, etc. No matter what someone else has done, we're not entitled to stay in these negative emotions. It takes us out of alignment with God and with the people around us.

> "Therefore, if you are offering your gift at the altar and there remember that your brother or sister has something against you, leave your gift there in front of the altar. First go and be reconciled to them; then come and offer your gift."
>
> MATTHEW 5:23-24

We also need to forgive those who have hurt us, like we talked about in chapter 6. This includes both forgiving people for what they've done and also for all of the negative consequences of their actions. Then bless them. This forgiveness process will heal you and free you for God to speak and work in a greater way.

Ask God for Healing: Once you've gone through repenting and forgiving, then you may have the healing that you need. But sometimes the healing involves more components and goes deeper. For example, you may have a hurt from when you were younger that requires healing, or a fear that God wants to take away, or an insecurity about yourself or your abilities that needs to be calmed. When I know what specifically needs to be healed, I do ask God for that particular healing. But sometimes I have no clue what's wrong, I simply know that I'm having a very strong negative emotion. When I find myself in that situation, I simply ask God to heal whatever in me needs to be healed. Sometimes He lets me know exactly what He's healing. Other times He just does the work without explaining what happened. I know the healing is done when I no longer feel the strong negative emotion when I think about the person or situation. The trigger is gone.

If Appropriate, Talk to the Other Person: If you've been hurt by something someone did or didn't do, it can be appropriate to talk with him about how the situation made you feel after you've done the above work. Don't blame him but explain your perspective and what you would appreciate him doing or not doing in the future. Also, if there is something you did to contribute to the situation, own it, apologize, and explain how you want to choose to act differently in the future.

Authentic, open, honest communication with people who are willing to listen and to respond in healthy ways can be very healing. However, as a caveat, if you had a feeling like envy toward someone, it's rarely helpful to share. Not liking people simply because of who they are, particularly their good qualities, is not their fault. Not only will this not help you but also you'll end up hurting other people.

Asking God to heal you so that you can respond more calmly will allow you to get and stay in right relationship with other people. In turn this will allow you to align your time with all the good God has for you because you're not caught in negative emotional cycles or relational drama.

■ ■ ■

Guarding Your Heart: Be Wise as Serpents and Innocent as Doves

In terms of guarding your heart, always start with yourself first. The majority of the time if you have an issue with someone—and particularly if you have an issue with many someones—you're the issue. Let go of worry and let God heal you, and so much in your life can calm down. You'll naturally be in right relationship with God and people most of the time and freed to invest your life in activities that will bless you and others.

However, and this is a *very* important however, not everything is your fault, and some people are legitimately dysfunctional and/or malicious.

I'm someone whose natural tendency is to assume the best of others and to also take responsibility for situations. In many ways that's good, but at times, it's not. I've had to learn more about the concept of being as wise as a serpent while also innocent as a dove.

> *"I am sending you out like sheep among wolves. Therefore be as shrewd as snakes and as innocent as doves."*
> MATTHEW 10:16

What this means is that sometimes having right relationship with a person and experiencing the best life God has for you means no relationship at all or a relationship with really good boundaries. This can feel especially tricky within a church setting because we're called to love our brothers and sisters in Christ. In general, we assume that it's a safe environment. But even in church, you can come across psychologically disturbed people, and these people can take advantage of supersweet people if they're not shrewd as serpents in addition to being as innocent as doves.

If you're in a situation where you've done the work on yourself and things still feel off, here are a few principles that can help you discern next steps.

Trust Your Gut: If you feel unsafe, there's a good chance that something is wrong. Particularly pay attention if the feeling of lack of safety comes in the form of a physical response—hives, tension, headache, pit in your stomach, etc. Your body is often a better indicator of your true feelings than your conscious mind. Also, take note if you feel a need to do something differently around a person than you would typically instinctively do. For example, feeling a need to lock a door, not wanting to be alone with her, or feeling uncomfortable discussing something that you would typically have no problem talking about with others.

Notice Patterns: Another way to tell if it's not you but the other person is to take note of patterns. Does this other person have a history of conflict with others? Does she have few relationships or relationships with lots of drama? Does she talk frequently about how other people are so mean to her or haven't treated her right? If someone has a pattern of dysfunctional relationships, that person is the common denominator. I'm not a fan of gossip so I'm not encouraging talking about people behind their backs all the time. But if you are in a situation where you think you see a pattern and believe someone may be a true danger to your community, please speak up to the appropriate people. Abuse happens when everyone is being so nice that no one protects the sheep from the wolves. That's not being nice, that's being foolish.

Be OK with No Relationship: As Christians we are called to be kind to others, but we're not called to be close with everyone.

Even Jesus had an inside circle and others that weren't so close to Him. If you feel unsafe and uncomfortable with someone and have a sense that something is off with him, it's OK to let go of a relationship. Oftentimes by simply stopping putting effort into a relationship, it will fade away. But other times, you'll need to set a firmer boundary. For example, you may need to decline invitations to do things one-on-one with a person, or you may choose not to talk with him about personal topics. You can choose to leave small-group settings where you need to interact with this person. You can also say no to certain requests for help from a person if you feel that your boundaries are being violated. You are called to help people, but most important you're meant to be in alignment with God's will. If God is not calling you to do something, you don't need to do it, particularly when it involves someone who is potentially abusive or manipulative.

When in doubt, one of the easiest ways to say no to someone is to say that you prayed about it and you don't have peace. Case closed without having to give a further *because*.

By being wise as serpents and innocent as doves, we can save ourselves tons of time and heartache, stay in right relationship with others, and enter into God's best.

Guarding Your Heart: Use the Jesus Shield

Over the years, I've learned to set good boundaries. But one of the difficulties with setting boundaries with people, particularly people who don't have a great deal of respect for boundaries, is that it can be difficult to be both firm and tenderhearted.

Fortunately, God gave me some insight about how to do both because good boundaries are extremely important for healthy relationships, good time management, and a happy, healthy me.

Without good boundaries, I can end up agitated, resentful, angry, and even sick. My body literally has an allergic reaction when I let unhealthy people invade my space. (As a side note, a lot of skin ailments are caused by fear of other people and allowing certain individuals to be closer to you than is good for you. As you set better boundaries, eczema, psoriasis, hives, and other issues may completely clear up.)

Because of this knowledge, I've chosen to set many more boundaries with individuals. I've also let go of a lot of friendships and activities that God told me weren't healthy for me anymore. I did this out of obedience to the Lord and knowledge that it was right, but some part of me still felt bad about "cutting people off."

My preferred state of being is openhearted, kind, and connected. So when I set boundaries, it can make me feel uncomfortable. I know the same can be true for many of you.

That's why I want to share an image God gave me that helped me reframe my perspective on the dynamic when I set boundaries with others.

In this image, I saw Jesus standing between me and the person making the unhealthy bid for connection with me. Jesus was holding a shield of grace. That shield of grace deflected the unhealthy bid for connection with me up to God and translated it into a cry for help. God then sent down healing upon that person.

At the same time, Jesus was praying for the person and I also could pray for the person. Our prayers could be completely loving and openhearted and accelerate the other person's healing without having any negative toll on us because our interaction was with God the Father, not with the person making the unhealthy bid for time, attention, or connection.

Through this vision, I could clearly see that I could stay completely kind and openhearted and bless people, even while setting boundaries with others. The key is allowing Jesus to be my protector and trusting God to take care of people through my prayer instead of feeling like I need to protect myself or interact directly with the person.

I hope that this insight is as freeing to you as it was for me! You can both have very healthy boundaries and be very kind.

I encourage you to think through any current situations where you may need to employ the shield of grace and start using it within those interactions. This will save you so much stress and time because you'll no longer be holding up shields yourself, and you will come through situations unharmed.

I appreciate how Melody Beattie in *The New Codependency* words it:

> Boundaries aren't something we just "get." They come from inside of us as honest expressions of who we are. At first setting limits is hard, but it becomes easier with practice and time. We open our mouths and say what we mean instead of saying what we think people want to hear.
>
> Boundaries are the limits of love.[29]

Right relationship with others plays a huge role in our having alignment with God with our time. When you live a life where

---

[29] Melody Beattie, *The New Codependency: Help and Guidance For Today's Generation* (New York: Simon & Schuster, 2009), 25.

you cultivate love by being giving, peacemaking, intentional, and vulnerable, you grow the depth and richness of relationships. When you guard your heart in your relationships through worrying less, pointing the finger at yourself, being wise as a serpent and innocent as a dove, and using the Jesus shield, you protect and preserve your connections with others. We want to invest our time in making positive deposits in our relationships instead of stressing about them.

Then, the final element of alignment with God with our time is having a right relationship with ourselves, which we'll explore in the next chapter. Jesus tells us to love others as ourselves, so to love others well, we need to love ourselves well.

Reflection Exercise: GIVING UP CONTROL

Whenever you try to get your needs met through control, you end up being controlled and addicted. You lose your freedom. You enter into bondage that prevents the pain you are trying to self-medicate from ever being healed.

We were made to have our needs met through relationships with people we don't control. Love—a free choice— is the only thing that will satisfy our hearts.

This is why the counterfeits never live up to their promises. This is why all of us must face our fear of rejection, be healed of shame, and risk our hearts in relationships. We must be willing to offer the truth of who we are to those we love, and receive the truth of who they are. Only the truth can make us free.[30]

—Danny Silk, *Keep Your Love On!*

---

[30] Danny Silk, *Keep Your Love On! Connection, Communication & Boundaries* (Redding, CA: Loving On Purpose, 2013), 104.

When I read this quote, I immediately sensed the power of it. Just like control isn't the goal with our lives, control isn't the goal with other people. In fact anyone or anything that we allow to control us is an idol, a counterfeit god. We want our relationships to be based on real, unconditional love where others meet our needs out of love for us, not because they feel they have to.

Take some time to evaluate whether or not you're living from a place of control and trying to get people to do things for you, or from a place of mutual love, trust, and respect.

One way to know that you're operating out of a place of control is that you feel anxious anytime you believe people may not do something in the way that you want them to do it. You tell yourself, "I cannot be happy if [this person] does/does not do [this action]." Because of this fear of losing control, you then do everything you can to ensure the other person acts in a certain way.

To break out of this control pattern, you'll need to practice putting your security in God instead of in what others do or do not do. Then, you'll need to speak your truth about what you want or need and give others a freewill choice to decide how they will or will not respond. You'll also need to get to the place of recognizing that no matter what other people choose to do or not do, you'll be OK. God will provide.

In my experience, there is always more than enough love in my life if I open myself up to give and receive love freely without rigid rules on how, when, and from whom it should come. When I'm completely open to experiencing love from God Himself and from whomever He puts in my path, the flow of love never stops.

★ ★ ★

This shift in your approach will make a massive difference in your peace and can also bring about the best results in your relationships.

God's best,
Elizabeth

There is no fear in love. But perfect love drives out fear
because fear has to do with punishment. The one who fears is
not made perfect in love.
We love because He first loved us.

1 JOHN 4:18–19

CHAPTER 8

Right Relationship with Ourselves

For no one ever hated his own flesh, but nourishes and cherishes it, just as Christ also does the church.

EPHESIANS 5:29 NASB

When we're younger, we go through phases where we want to have or be whatever we're not. If we have straight hair, we want curly hair. If we have curly hair, we want straight hair. If we're short, we want to be tall. If we're tall, we want to be short.

But then a blissful shift happens when we decide to accept and embrace who we are. All of a sudden, everything becomes easier. We stop worrying about trying to look like someone we're not and allow ourselves to be the best version of ourselves.

The breakthrough I had was this: in the same way that we must learn to love ourselves to enjoy the richest life possible, we must learn to love our story line.

So much angst in life is caused by thinking, "I'm too old, I should be further along in my career, in my family, in [this or that achievement]." Or, "I'm too young, I shouldn't have all this responsibility yet, I'm missing out on my life, I'm not ready for this, everything is happening too fast."

The truth is that your unique story line is just right for you.

★ ★ ★

Nothing is wrong when your life doesn't look exactly like someone else's. Quite the opposite is true: if your story line looks exactly like someone's or many someones', that's a bad sign that you're conforming yourself to a mold instead of allowing the beautiful distinctness of who God made you to come forth.

This revelation holds special significance when you're thinking about goals and plans.

Letting go of forcing your story line is at its core about stopping to try to make your life look how you think it "should" be and allowing it to be what truly resonates with your truest self. Signs you're forcing include:

- Little to no progress
- Little to no desire to change but feeling guilty about that lack of desire to change, so you keep goals on your list anyway
- Lack of satisfaction when you do what you think you "should do" or have what you think you "should have"
- Constantly feeling deprived, which leads to distracting yourself with unsatisfying pursuits

For some of you, it's time to ditch some of those perennial goals to change yourself or change your life in a way that "seems right" but doesn't *feel* right.

Letting go of forcing is a vulnerable act because you're releasing the sense of control you have from perpetually pursuing concrete, socially acceptable objectives. But that openness can allow the real you to emerge and help you come into right relationship with your true self.

This right relationship with yourself then leads to peace and alignment with God's best.

SELF-LOVE WITHOUT SELF-CENTEREDNESS

I understand that by suggesting right relationship with ourselves as part of our alignment with God that I'm walking on delicate theological ground. Some Christian camps will fall more on the absolutely-love-yourself-all-the-time side of the spectrum and others will err more toward the deny-yourself-of-everything end.

As for me, I'm aware that we're not supposed to love our lives:

> "For whoever wants to save their life will lose it, but whoever loses their life for me and for the gospel will save it."
>
> (Mark 8:35)

And we're not supposed to love the things of the world:

> Do not love the world or anything in the world. If anyone loves the world, love for the Father is not in them. For everything in the world—the lust of the flesh, the lust of the eyes, and the pride of life—comes not from the Father but from the world. The world and its desires pass away, but whoever does the will of God lives forever.
>
> (1 John 2:15–17)

But God clearly tells us that we are deeply loved, lovable, and worthy:

"For God so loved the world that He gave His only
begotten Son, that whosoever believeth in Him should
not perish, but have everlasting life."

(John 3:16 KJ21)

"Since you are precious and honored in my sight, and
because I love you, I will give people in exchange for you,
nations in exchange for your life."

(Isaiah 43:4)

And the benchmark of how we are supposed to love others is
our love for ourselves:

"Do not seek revenge or bear a grudge against anyone
among your people, but love your neighbor as yourself. I
am the LORD."

(Leviticus 19:18)

In this same way, husbands ought to love their wives as
their own bodies. He who loves his wife loves himself.
After all, no one ever hated their own body, but they feed
and care for their body, just as Christ does the church.

(Ephesians 5:28–29)

So from my vantage point, an essential part of aligning with
God's plans for our lives is to love ourselves in the way that God
wants us to love ourselves. That's right relationship with yourself. In this chapter, we'll explore how to practice healthy self-
acceptance and self-compassion; spiritual, physical, emotional,
and mental self-care; and self-discovery.

This includes avoiding the extremes of controlling yourself through over-regimenting everything and trying to be perfect, as well as the opposite unhealthy extreme of complete self-indulgence.

Despite what popular culture says, both excessive self-control and excessive self-indulgence are violence against yourself. Healthy self-acceptance, self-care, and self-discovery are about being true to yourself. This frees you to take your attention off of yourself and to love God and others with everything you do and everything you are and everything you have.

My heart's desire is that we will all overflow with an abundance of time, energy, resources, and most of all love, so that overflow can bless as many people as possible this side of heaven and bring as many people with us to the other side.

When our life is in order and our heart is focused on God and others, self fades away...

■   ■   ■

SELF-ACCEPTANCE AND SELF-COMPASSION

When sin entered the world, Adam and Eve hid themselves, and humans have been trying to hide themselves ever since.

As we covered in chapter 3, we can have lots of false identities that we hide behind as a way to earn love. In chapters 4 and 5, we went through how to know and love your true identity in Christ. In Christ we are dearly beloved, chosen, a royal priesthood and all other sorts of good things.

All of the really good stuff God says about us in Scripture is 100 percent true. But it's also true that until we get to heaven, we'll never be perfect. We have scars, wrinkles, and broken bits inside and outside of us. So what about that reality? How do we feel great about ourselves and resist the urge to hide when we know we're broken?

Here are some reflections from a variety of sources on self-acceptance and self-compassion and self-love in light of the fact that we can *all* be tempted to believe the lie that we have fatal flaws. Ask God to allow these to soak into your spirit so that you can truly not only accept but also have compassion and love for yourself in your weakness.

To start, it's essential to know that God is not turned off by your weakness. Similar to how your heart can move with compassion when you see a child or pet in distress, God feels that way about you:

> When the woman saw that the fruit of the tree was good for food and pleasing to the eye, and also desirable for gaining wisdom, she took some and ate it. She also gave some to her husband, who was with her, and he ate it. Then the eyes of both of them were opened, and they realized they were naked; so they sewed fig leaves together and made coverings for themselves.
>
> Then the man and his wife heard the sound of the Lord God as he was walking in the garden in the cool of the day, and they hid from the Lord God among the trees of the garden. But the Lord God called to the man, "Where are you?"
>
> He answered, "I heard you in the garden, and I was afraid because I was naked; so I hid."
>
> GENESIS 3:6-10

The Lord is close to the brokenhearted; he rescues those whose spirits are crushed.

(Psalm 34:18 NLT)

> For we have not a high priest, who can not have compassion on our infirmities: but one tempted in all things like as we are, without sin.
>
> (Hebrews 4:15 DRA)

> But he said to me, "My grace is sufficient for you, for my power is made perfect in weakness." Therefore I will boast all the more gladly about my weaknesses, so that Christ's power may rest on me. That is why, for Christ's sake, I delight in weaknesses, in insults, in hardships, in persecutions, in difficulties. For when I am weak, then I am strong.
>
> (2 Corinthians 12:9–11)

Let that really, really soak in. Make it a selah moment.

You don't need to put on your Sunday-best clothes and plaster a smile on your face to approach God. (Remember, no more plastic princess or prince.) God loves you best when you're just you. He loves that He can get the closest and deepest love relationship with you when you're broken and own up to it. He knows everything you're doing, experiencing, thinking, and feeling anyway so why try to hide it?

We aren't insecure or codependent to want to find the answer to our questions in the eyes of another: "Am I lovable?" "Am I worthy?" "Can I do it?" We're exactly how God made us. The key is that we need to look into God's eyes first for the answers to these questions. Only in Him will we never be alone, and the answer to all our questions always be yes. The Holy Spirit can do the transforming work of making us totally secure in Him no matter what others have or haven't done for us or continue to do or not do. That frees us to stop using our time to earn worth and simply to accept it.

A Japanese concept that encompasses this well is the idea of *wabi-sabi*. It's used in relation to objects like teacups or home furnishings, but I believe it also applies to how we perceive ourselves and our brokenness. Here's how the concept is explained in *The Wabi-Sabi House: The Japanese Art of Imperfect Beauty*: "To create serenity at home, wabi-sabi asks that we set aside our judgments and our longing for perfection and focus, instead, on the beauty of things as they are, at this very moment."[31]

Now Apply This to Yourself: To create serenity in myself and with myself, I set aside my judgments of myself and my longing for perfection and focus, instead, on the beauty and worthiness of myself as I am, at this very moment.

Then stop right there.

No thoughts about . . . *and I need to improve this about myself or I wish this were different.* Just *I focus on the beauty and worthiness of myself as I am, at this very moment.* Sit with that truth and allow God to let it sink into your bones.

Here's another exercise and perspective from *The New Codependency* that not only allows you to accept that you're worthy as you are but also to celebrate the good God can do in and through your brokenness:

Love yourself for your illnesses, disorders, or problems. If you haven't forgiven yourself for issues, problems,

---

[31] Robyn Griggs Lawrence, *The Wabi-Sabi House: The Japanese Art of Imperfect Beauty* (New York: Clarkson Potter, 2004), 10.

or illnesses, start using this affirmation or write one for yourself. I forgive, love, and accept myself for having _____ and/or _____. I'm grateful for the lessons these issues have taught me and the gifts they've given, and all I'm going to learn. Then look in the mirror—into your eyes. Say the words out loud three times daily for twenty-one days or until you know you're speaking the truth. It's easy to feel guilty for having issues like addictions or codependency, but it's time to forgive yourself.[32]

The above affirmation is very powerful, and looking into your eyes in the mirror is also very powerful—and very vulnerable. When I did this the first time, I started crying. There's something about looking into your eyes in the mirror (not as an act of vanity but an act of vulnerability) that helps you to be truly present to yourself and to your heart. It can stir up a grief around your self-rejection and hiding. That's natural and normal. If it becomes too much, you can stop. But just truly know that God didn't make any mistakes with you and He can redeem even the worst of situations. The healthiest attitude is to avoid self-condemnation and self-pity and instead to thank God for our struggles, for what we've learned from them, and for how our experience can benefit others. "And we know that God causes all things to work together for good to those who love God, to those who are called according to *His* purpose" (Rom. 8:28 NASB).

---

[32] Melody Beattie, *The New Codependency: Help and Guidance for Today's Generation* (New York: Simon & Schuster, 2009), 76.

WHY YOU MUST FIND LOVE WITHIN

*I talk in this book about some of the struggles of not being in
a relationship at certain times in my life. But I'm well aware
through my own experience and through an up-close-and-
personal look at many people's lives that being in a relationship
or marriage where you don't feel well loved can feel more
excruciatingly painful than being single. This is especially true
when you're looking for love exclusively from your partner
instead of recognizing that God can provide love for you in so
many different forms and from so many different sources.*

*Other people can and should be an expression of God's
love. It's a wonderful thing when they care for our hearts well.
And the individuals around us, especially our significant other,
can have a huge impact on our emotional, psychological, and
physical well-being. But no person—no matter how wonderful he
or she is—can be the ultimate source that we look to in order to
know we're loved. We must receive God's perfect, limitless love
and choose to love ourselves in order to experience the fullness
of love, joy, connection, and satisfaction our hearts desire.*

This sense of self-acceptance and self-compassion is essential
to not only having a right relationship with yourself but also
having a right relationship with other people and God. Here's
how Brené Brown puts it in *The Gifts of Imperfection: Let Go of
Who You Think You're Supposed to Be and Embrace Who You Are*:

Only *one thing* separated the men and women who felt a
deep sense of love and belonging from the people who
seem to be struggling for it. That one thing is the belief in
their worthiness. It's as simple and complicated as this: If

we want to fully experience love and belonging, we must believe that we are worthy of love and belonging.

When we can let go of what other people think and own our story, we gain access to our worthiness—the feeling that we are enough just as we are and that we are worthy of love and belonging.[33]

The time is now to embrace self-acceptance and self-compassion. It's the only way to enter into God's best with your life and your time, and the only thing holding you back from it is yourself.

NOT CONTROLLING YOURSELF, LOVING YOURSELF

Once you've embraced self-acceptance and self-compassion, you can truly enter into healthy self-care. Healthy self-care is not about controlling yourself, punishing yourself, or trying to make yourself fit into a mold of what seems "right" or "good." Healthy self-care is about attuning to your spiritual, physical, emotional, and mental needs. This attunement leads to right relationship with yourself because you're aware of and meeting your needs in the right ways and at the right times.

If you're feeling drained or resentful, it's likely that you need to invest in more self-care. And on the flip side, if your "self-care" goals seem burdensome, you might need to modify them

---

[33] Brené Brown, PhD, LMSW, *The Gifts of Imperfection: Let Go of Who You Think You're Supposed to Be and Embrace Who You Are* (Center City, MN: Hazelden, 2010), 23.

in terms of what you're doing, how often, or when so that they feel like self-love instead of self-torture. If it feels awful to you, it might be awful for you no matter what some infomercial star says. It's time to love yo'self.

Loving Yourself: Spiritual Self-Care

In chapters 2 and 6, we talked extensively about putting trust in God at the center of your life and growing love between you and God. These spiritual disciplines are great ways to take care of your spiritual life on a regular basis. But the spiritual self-care I want to cover here is a little bit different.

Basically, spiritual self-care involves staying aware of whether you're connected to or disconnected from God. Typically the easiest, most accurate indicator is the presence or absence of the fruit of the Spirit in your life. Galatians 5:22–23 lists them: "But the fruit of the Spirit is love, joy, peace, longsuffering, gentleness, goodness, faith, meekness, temperance: against such there is no law" (kjv).

If you're experiencing those fruits, then most likely you are connected to God. But if you're not experiencing love, joy, peace, patience, gentleness, goodness, faith, humility, and self-control, then most likely there's a block between you and God. That will leave you feeling afraid, anxious, lonely, and typically ungrateful.

Spiritual self-care involves staying aware of that connection. Then when you have a sense that a block may be present, give yourself what you need to get unblocked. In some ways, this is about your relationship with God. But at its core, spiritual self-care is about your relationship with yourself and meeting your spiritual needs. God is never blocked, it's you and me that get off track. Investing time in reconnecting with God is the highest and best use of our time because it is the root cause of lack of peace. So when we invest time in restoring the love relationship between God and ourselves, our hearts will find rest.

These spiritual self-care needs may vary widely, even on a moment-by-moment basis. Sometimes they will "fit the mold" and other times they may look very different than normal. Here are just a few ideas of what you may need in regard to spiritual self-care to regain your connection with God. You can use these as a jumping-off point. But ultimately you need to pay attention to what your spirit is saying it needs at any particular time:

Longer Times with God: This could look like a walk in the woods, turning off all noise when you commute, going to a coffee shop for an evening, or taking a day off of work to just be with God. It could look like more time in the Word, more time meditating, more time journaling, more time reading spiritual books, more time praying, or more time with whatever else you believe you need to get beyond surface connection with God to in-depth connection. Sometimes our normal spiritual routines just aren't enough.

New Worship Experience: During some seasons, you'll need to make changes in your worship experience with others. That may mean switching the church service time you attend, going to a different church, going to multiple churches, going to worship experiences not connected with a church, listening to more worship and teachings online, or not going to church at all for a while and using that time to do more worship on your own or with a smaller group of people. I do believe that God wants us to meet with others and that having an ongoing church community is important. But if you feel disconnected from God, sometimes you need to shake things up in your worship experience to get reconnected.

Time Away: Sometimes what you need the most is time away outside of your normal day-to-day routine to hit the reset button. This could look like a night away at a retreat center. Or you may want to go to a conference or consider a special program. A big turning point in my life was when I did a forty-day Christian leadership program in the woods of northern Minnesota in the summer of 2008. That time away from everything "normal" allowed God to completely change the trajectory of my life. Although in some ways it was a practical sacrifice—I needed to put my business on hold for that time—it has infinitely paid off spiritually and in many other ways. It was a great investment of time in putting God first. I have no regrets.

Support from Others: There are times to give and there are also times to receive. Particularly if you have a tendency toward giving, it's essential that you have some people in your life who can give you spiritual support. Sometimes this looks like someone in a formal position. For example, getting spiritual support and direction from a pastor, priest, or other leader in your faith community. Other times, there are people in churches or other religious groups trained in prayer ministry or Christ-centered support like Stephen Ministers, laypeople trained to give one-on-one care to hurting people (www.stephenminis tries.org). Still other times, God will gift you with mentors and friends who will be able to provide this support in less formal ways. I treasure the many beautiful people God has serendipitously brought into my life who speak life and truth into me on a regular basis.

When you engage in these types of relationships, it's good to look for someone whom you can trust who's not critical and not enabling. You shouldn't be looking to them to solve your problems, make decisions for you, and definitely not control or rescue you, but instead to walk alongside you in the process, pray for you, remind you of the truth of God's Word and of God's love for you. There may be times where you don't need to talk to someone like this for months and other times where you need weekly or even daily support.

Get Really Honest: Finally, at times, you don't need something big or epic to change outside of yourself; instead, you need an internal shift to reconnect with God. For example, maybe you need to forgive someone, stop doing a sin and repent, get honest with God about how you're mad at Him, or let go of expectations about how you or your life "should" be. Or maybe you need to think back to a time in your past when you felt connected with God and use that experience to foster those feelings again and to practice intentional gratitude.

One of the best questions to ask yourself to test whether or not you're being totally honest about your connection with God is this one: Can I look God in the eyes? If you can, you're usually fully transparent. If you can't, then there's typically some area of your life where you need to open up to God more.

You'll know you've unblocked the barrier between you and God when you start to feel the fruits of the Spirit again. Often this is accompanied by tears because something released inside of you, and you typically will start to feel more peace almost immediately.

If you can't get to this place or don't know if you ever have experienced this type of connection, there is a ministry built around Emmanuel prayer to create and restore that connection with God. You can find more resources at www.immanuel approach.com.

The biggest key with spiritual self-care is to stay attuned with what you need. You might not have a rational explanation for your choices, and it may not make sense to others. But when your spirit says, "Yes, I need that," give it to yourself. Then observe how the experience has an impact on your sense of connection with God. Oftentimes you will just need to do one of the above things for a season. Then you can go back to your normal routines and still remain connected and aligned with God.

■ ■ ■

Loving Yourself: Physical Self-Care

Almost everyone knows taking care of your health is a good idea. But many people don't take care of their bodies, because it "makes sense" on a mental level but feels like self-deprivation more than self-love on an emotional level. Sitting on the couch eating potato chips until past midnight feels like a luxurious indulgence . . . until the next morning.

So how do you make investing time in taking care of the basics, like sleep, exercise, and eating, really seem like self-care? One way is to become more conscious of how what you do—or don't do—has an impact on how you feel. For example, if you realize that when you go to bed after midnight, you can't focus the next day and feel awful at work, you can see going to bed before midnight as an act of self-love. You may not feel like stepping away from your computer at eleven thirty p.m. to wind down. But you know that if you do and give up the relatively small pleasure from the extra hour of Internet surfing and TV watching until twelve thirty a.m., you'll feel so much better all of the next day. The recognition of how your choices have an impact on you can help you make better choices—and not resent them.

The same goes for exercising. Some people enjoy the process of exercise. That makes it easier for them to just do it. But for others, you need to think about the positive benefits that come from exercise like having more energy, feeling less stiff, sleeping better, and having a better mood. This can shift your focus from exercise being something you "have" to do to exercise being something you want to do with your time. Finding physical activity you really enjoy can help too. Consider playing a sport, taking a class, dancing, running around with your kids, volunteering with Habitat for Humanity, or doing anything else that gets you moving and gives you pleasure.

Another way that you can turn physical self-care into something that actually feels like self-love to you is to focus on something called "attunement." The idea of attuned eating was brought to my attention by Sarah Grace of Fresh Fit N Healthy, and Tracy Brown, RD, a nutrition therapist. I'm far from an expert on this topic. You can find more at freshfitnhealthy.com and www.tracybrownrd.com. But I can tell you that in my personal experience this approach to eating has completely transformed my relationship with food, weight, and my body.

> *I love how Tracy Brown, a nutrition therapist, put this truth about letting go of numbers so beautifully. I think her words apply in all areas, not just body image:*
>
> *Decoding the desire to be thin decreases the suffering of pursuing thinness (or other desired body change) and opens you up to your heart and soul.* Pursuing thinness leaves our true desires and needs un-heard—that is the real cost.[34]

For most of my life, I've been slender, so when I learned about attuned eating, I wasn't concerned about losing weight. But what was revolutionary about this concept was my approach toward maintaining a healthy weight. I reached my full height when I was eleven years old. So by the time I was thirteen years old, I started to pay close attention to my weight because I could no longer eat whatever, whenever and not put on pounds. My freshman year of high school, I got superthin. Not quite at the eating disorder level but heading in that direction. At that point in my life, I put a tremendous amount of pressure on myself to be perfect and to be in control. Being hyper-regimented in what I ate and exercising a ton were ways to "calm" my fear about gaining weight. I wasn't thinking about how to be healthy and happy. I was thinking, "Fat is bad, and I don't want to be fat." In that process, I learned how to override my body's hunger signals through self-discipline. Fortunately my superthin phase didn't last too long, and I was back up to a healthy weight by age fifteen.

Since then, except for a year when I gained and lost about

---

[34] Tracy Brown, e-mail on January 24, 2017.

thirty pounds, I've been in about the same weight range. Part of how I stayed in the same weight range was through weekly weigh-in times. Each Friday, I would weigh myself and record the number. If I had gained some weight, I would look to pull back my eating in the coming week. If I was underweight, I'd give myself more permission to splurge. If I knew a time of indulgence was coming up, like a holiday, I would cut back so that I could eat whatever I wanted at that time. Also if I felt uncertain about my weight for whatever reason, I would weigh myself more frequently.

Overall, I felt this system worked very well for me since it effectively gave me the external results that I wanted for about twenty years. But in 2016, God asked me to make a shift toward the way of attuned eating. One of the ways He asked me to do that was to cut back to weighing myself only once a month. Also, the focus was to go from "eating healthy" or "being a certain weight" to giving my body what it wanted when it wanted it. That meant eating when I was hungry, not eating when I wasn't hungry, and stopping when I was full. I've been following this way of interacting with food and my body since the beginning of 2016.

The first couple of weeks, I felt really nervous. I could tell I gained a little weight, because my clothes fit a bit tighter. I worried that I would keep putting on pounds. But I reminded myself that in this area God was teaching me that self-love was more important than self-control. I could love and accept myself at any weight, and I was "Elizabeth," not a certain number on the scale.

Over time, what surprised me about this new way of being was that I didn't keep gaining weight. In fact my body went right back to the same range that it had been in before. Despite my lack of trust in my body previously, I discovered that I was enough in tune with my hunger and fullness signals that my body really did know what it needed when it needed it and could self-regulate. I didn't and don't need to "control" my eating or weigh myself all the time. I just need to love myself through food, and it works out. This has produced a more peaceful relationship between myself and my body, which allows me to have right relationship with myself.

On her website, Tracy goes into lots of details about how to get in tune with your body's hunger and fullness signals. I know that won't come as easily to everyone as it happened to come to me. But I can tell you that it is a very free way to live. Although you can't see much of a difference on the outside of me with my new way of approaching food, I can feel a huge difference on the inside. Weight and food—something that used to consume a much larger part of my mental space—are now simply parts of my life that flow without my really needing to think about them. In fact, it's so rare for me to think about these topics that when I feel an urge to weigh myself or find myself going through a mental list of what I ate throughout the day, that's a sign to me that I'm feeling out of control for some reason. I don't need to waste time worrying about food but instead ask myself what's bothering me.

Truly aligned physical self-care involves giving yourself what you want or need to enter into all the blessings that God wants you to experience. That includes remembering what makes you feel good in the end, even if it might not be what you feel like doing in the beginning. And it involves tuning in with what you really need at each moment—whether it's a cookie, a nap, or a walk outside.

Finally, for those who see investing time in physical self-care as selfish or unspiritual, here's what God has to say about the topic:

> Do you not know that your bodies are temples of the
> Holy Spirit, who is in you, whom you have received from
> God? You are not your own; you were bought at a price.
> Therefore honor God with your bodies.
>
> (1 Corinthians 6:19–20)

This passage is specifically about sexual immorality, but I believe that it can apply to all the ways you do or don't take care of your body. It matters. It's not selfish or wrong to love yourself through physical self-care.

Loving Yourself: Emotional Self-Care

Emotions happen. Moment by moment. Day by day. Month by month. Year by year.

I've heard emotions described as energy. But I think that they're more than that. They're the voices of our inner selves. Not always our most holy selves, but our inner selves, nonetheless. It's important to give yourself permission to feel. As one of my close friends Lynne May so wisely told me, "I encourage you to be gentle and compassionate with yourself and to know it is acceptable to be exactly where you are in the moment. God is there, Emmanuel."[35]

By paying attention to your emotions and taking time to attend to them, you can enter into God's best in your life and bring your best to the world. During my morning quiet time,

---

[35] Lynne May, text message to the author, January 3, 2017.

I give myself permission to do a lot of thinking, praying, and journaling. This daily practice allows me to do an emotional cleanse of sorts. The goal is to clear out anything that's bothering me and give it to God so that I can approach the day from a healthy, centered place. The act of expression and surrender to God often takes care of the emotion, simply because I get it out and put it in the hands of the One who can actually do something about it. I also find that when I take things to God in prayer, He sometimes gives me new insights on what to do or how to think about something that is bothering me.

On the flip side, if I don't give myself permission to express my emotions to God through prayer and journaling on a daily basis, I can end up with a backlog of negative energy below the surface in my life. Because of how God made me, taking time for this practice is essential for my emotional health. For others it's not as important. Instead some people may find talking to others most helpful or thinking things through without actually writing anything down or saying anything. Know yourself and what you need to have an emotionally healthy life.

> *Don't forget the heart-body connection when thinking about emotional self-care. Sometimes what you need to feel good is less talking and more exercising, especially outside. Or if you live far from the equator, you may need some extra vitamin D or a sun lamp in winter. Our emotional pain can be an expression of physical pain and vice versa. Look for the links.*

Daily emotional self-care is to your heart what taking a shower is to your body. It keeps you clean and relatively pleasant to be around. But sometimes you experience emotional wounds that

> Give all your worries and
> cares to God, for he cares
> about you.
>
> 1 PETER 5:7 NLT

need a bit more attention: you get slighted by a friend, you have a coworker say something nasty, a family member yells at you, or something else happens that causes you to feel hurt, angry, insecure, or afraid. In those cases, you've incurred an emotional injury. You need to give it extra attention in the same way you would give a physical wound special, usually immediate care.

The same techniques that work on a daily basis, such as praying, journaling, or talking to someone, can work for these special circumstances too. But often you need some extra time to do the emotional processing. If you're really worked up, you may need to also do something to calm your body first. This could look like deep breathing or going on a run. These activities help get some of the strength of the emotional energy out of your body before you try to think things through.

You may also need to go through some of the techniques I cover in chapter 7 in the "Point the Finger...At Yourself" section to uncover and ask God to heal trigger points.

Emotional wounds matter. If we process and allow God to heal them, then we can move forward in our lives. But if we do not address emotional wounds, then they can fester below the surface. They will cause pain and problems for us and for others when the Band-Aids get pulled off.

Finally, at times we have more than a surface injury: a deep, potentially old emotional trauma. It could be an emotional cancer of anger or perhaps an acute injury like an emotional broken bone from a relationship gone wrong. This could lead you to seek out more extensive support like a therapist or counselor, or to attend a program on emotional healing. For example, in 2007,

I went through a program called the Ultimate Journey (www .theultimatejourney.org), at the time known as the Christ-Life Solution. In this program, you learn how to process through your life from infancy to the present and to replace the lies of the past with God's truth. All of us have ways that we've been injured, big and small. It's important to uncover and heal those areas so that we can move forward from a place of strength. There are many other ministries that can help with healing and deliverance, such as Unbound ministries (www.heartofthe father.com) and Sozo ministries (www.bethelsozo.com).

There are also programs that help you with not only processing the past but also learning the relational skills that you may not have learned along the way, such as having the ability to return to joy after you experience a negative emotion or knowing how to ask for what you want and need. One of these programs is known as Thrive training (https://joystartshere.com/thrivetraining/). This program combines the best information from brain science, counseling, and biblical teaching to understand how to learn the skills and receive the experiences that you never had so that you can live from a place of joy and emotional maturity.

Look into different resources and then pray about which is the right fit for you. God will lead you to the right people and resources at the right time if you're simply open to Him.

When you give yourself the time to acknowledge what you feel and ask God to help you understand and release your feelings, you'll end up in a better emotional place, act in a less emotional manner with others, and allow others to feel what they're feeling. Often if you can't tolerate an emotion in someone else, it means that it's an emotion that you can't tolerate in yourself. It's time to let God in so that the wounds can be uncovered, healed, and the pain released. Sometimes that's as simple as saying to God, "Please hold me," and allowing yourself to feel whatever you're feeling while you're held tight and safe in His arms. Other times it means a more formal and longer amount of support. But know that God has a greater longing for your healing than you do. He will do whatever it takes to heal and redeem any emotional wound in your life if you let Him. This will free you to enter into His best.

Loving Yourself: Mental Self-Care

> *Do not conform to the pattern of this world, but be transformed by the renewing of your mind. Then you will be able to test and approve what God's will is—his good, pleasing and perfect will.*

> ROMANS 12:2

Romans 12:2 talks about us being transformed by the renewing of our minds, i.e., as we change our thoughts, then all of us naturally follows suit. There are an infinite number of ways you could take good care of your mind. Ultimately, God will need to lead you on what you most need at any particular moment. Here we'll cover three areas in particular that are key to mental self-care.

The first is to pay attention to what you put into your mind. I'm not saying that you can only listen to Christian music and sermons all day long. But what I am saying is that it's so important to pay attention to how input helps or hurts you mentally. For example, you may want to limit how much time you spend watching or reading the news because it's purposely designed to fill you with fear. Or if there are certain other materials that cause you to sin by making you focus on the things of the world, like getting more power, lust, etc., you may want to stay away from them. This is why I need to be careful about how much time I invest in self-help or business advice. It's not necessarily intrinsically evil, but it's not always good for my soul.

Everything you watch or listen to makes an impression on your brain. The more impressions that are about truth and focus on the Lord, the more your brain will go in that direction. I purposely listen to praise music most of the day—sometimes I even do my exercise to it—so that I can constantly be filled with thoughts from the Lord. It's hard to think bad thoughts when your brain is full of good ones.

The second component of mental self-care I'll highlight is the epidemic of stimulus addiction. Because of modern technology, from the Internet to e-mail to mobile phones to social media to everything, you rarely have a time where you don't have access to some sort of random stimulation. If someone hasn't sent you a text message or e-mail since the last time you checked, you can always turn to your trusty random-new-information-provider Facebook for some fresh input. It's not easy to avoid the temptation to check technology, even for people like me who have a natural tendency toward being focused. Often there's a pull to do something else other than what we really need and want to do at the moment.

Even while I've been writing this chapter, I've felt the pull of wanting to check e-mail. Not because I'm actually waiting for something, just because. When I really need to focus and really want to reduce temptation, I turn off the sound on my phone so I can't hear calls or texts, and I close my e-mail tabs.

I find eliminating visual and audio prompts particularly important when I'm in a place of feeling afraid or insecure for whatever reason. When I'm generally uneasy, I tend to have a larger pull toward distraction. Owning up to the fact that I'm feeling anxious and taking the time to address the real emotional issue leads to the best results. Once I'm in a calm place, the temptation generally fades. Plus I get the added bonus of getting more connected to myself and God.

The third component of mental self-care I'll cover of this decidedly nonextensive list is refusing to come into agreement with lies. In short, the devil hates you and is constantly trying to feed you lies about God, about yourself, and about others. The worst part is that you often believe them and come into agreement with them. Then you live your life based on these lies instead of the truth of God's Word.

It grieves my spirit when I realize that certain wrong ways of thinking that I picked up from as young as infancy have kept me from living the life God wants me to live. It's painful when these lies come into my consciousness. But when I recognize the deception and see it for the lie that it is, there's hope because I have the possibility for change.

To start in this process of lie detection, know that anything that attacks who you are and tells you that you're unworthy, unlovable, shameful, etc., is just not of God. In Christ you are a beloved child of God, and no attacks on your identity are valid.

See what great love the Father has lavished on us, that we should be called children of God! And that is what we are!

(1 John 3:1a)

Also, any attacks on your destiny telling you that you have no purpose or your life doesn't matter or what you do is meaningless are also automatically false, wrong, invalid, and just plain ridiculous. We'll talk more about your life journey in the next section. But for now, just know that your life matters, and not only can you do something but also God has wonderful plans in mind for you.

> For we are God's masterpiece. He has created us anew in
> Christ Jesus, so we can do the good things he planned for
> us long ago.
>
> (Ephesians 2:10 NLT)

No matter what anyone told you or you told yourself, you and your life are not a mistake or an accident. No part of you is wrong, and there is nothing that can't be redeemed from your past. Even if all you can do is lie in bed and pray, your life matters…immensely. You don't need to prove or earn your worth. You just have it because you're God's child. If you're in God's will, you can experience His goodness in whatever situation you are in right here, right now. You are not an object of pity. You are more than a conqueror in Christ.

So what should you do when those lies inevitably come into your head? There's extensive material on this in the book *The Worry Free Life: Take Control of Your Thought Life by Weeding Out the Bad and Nurturing the Good!*, which is faith based, and in the book *Feeling Good: The New Mood Therapy*, which is a more general psychology book. But as a very quick crash course, the first step is to recognize when a lie comes into your head. If you recognize it immediately, you can then immediately reject the thought and for extra good measure "return it to sender." For some people it helps to think of the lies being bound to the cross of Christ. Then think about the truth. If it helps, read through Bible verses about your identity or other Christ-centered truths.

If you've already come into agreement with a lie, especially for a long time, you'll need to state that you break agreement with the lie, repent for having believed the lie, and ask God to fill you with His truth.

* * *

This process takes time. It's important that you invite God into the journey. He has the power to renew and transform your mind into the mind of Christ as you let Him. Your job is to be open and honest about your struggles and thoughts and to stand up to the lies. In Christ you are victorious, and you don't need to put up with these attacks. It's absolutely essential that you fight back and refuse to accept the negative thoughts that come into your head. God's job is to bring about the transformation that only He can do. Remember, similar to emotions—it's OK to admit that you have a bad thought or many bad thoughts—God can handle it. Just fess up and then let God do His work to heal your mind.

> Finally, brothers and sisters, whatever is true, whatever is noble, whatever is right, whatever is pure, whatever is lovely, whatever is admirable—if anything is excellent or praiseworthy—think about such things.
>
> PHILIPPIANS 4:8

This is a very non-comprehensive list but hopefully gives you a start of understanding how to take care of your mind so that it's aligned with God's truth and leads you into God's best.

■ ■ ■

NOT CONTROLLING YOUR LIFE, LOVING YOUR LIFE

Writing this entire book has been a spiritual journey for me. One that forces me in my public voice, not just in private, to acknowledge and embrace the limits of our human abilities to control our lives. It's humbling, vulnerable, real.

But in particular, this section is the hardest for me to write. That's probably why God had me put it last.

At the beginning of this chapter, I shared some "practical" advice from a newsletter I had sent to my subscribers. (You can join in the Real Life E inner circle at www.ScheduleMakeover .com.) What I wrote in this newsletter is good advice, if I do say so myself. It's important to note that your expectations about what would or wouldn't happen in your life often determine your happiness with your life, not what actually is or is not. A salary that might make you thrilled could make someone else cry or vice versa. Having a baby could be your sweetest dream and another person's nightmare. Our expectations make a profound difference in our experience of our life.

As I shared in chapter 3, I experienced many unexpected twists and turns professionally. But now looking back, I can see how my professional life has ended up so much better than I could have ever planned. I never intended to own a business but have been a full-time entrepreneur since 2005. I never planned to write, coach, or speak, but I've done all three all over the world. And for someone who never thought she would be an author, I'm now on my third book. This was a matter of life going off of charted territory and into God country. There were absolutely tears, disappointments, hard times financially, questioning God, and other sorts of struggles. But overall, sitting where I am now, it makes sense. I'm grateful for how God brought about plans in my life so much greater and better than I would have ever dreamed for myself.

But sometimes the answers aren't that clear...they don't come that fast...and they don't seem better than what you planned; they feel worse and even like God is punishing you or withholding from you.

Sometimes these parts of your story line involve bad things that have happened to you or are still happening to you now. Abuse happens. Addiction happens. Divorce happens. Poverty happens. Sickness happens. Death happens. There will be a time when God will wipe every tear from our eyes in heaven, but on this earth there is pain and there is suffering. It's a reality, and it doesn't always make sense and definitely doesn't always seem fair.

Sometimes these parts of your story line involve good things that haven't happened and aren't happening now. Maybe you want to finally move into the career that you believe is your calling but you're stuck and don't see a way out. Maybe you want to have a child and you haven't been able to have one. Maybe you want to be in a relationship and it just isn't working out. Maybe you've struggled with poverty for years and it seems impossible to ever get ahead.

I typically keep a firm line between my personal and professional life because I believe it's appropriate. I'm here to serve people who come to me as readers and clients, not to unload about what's going on with me. But I feel like God told me that to write this section as He intended that I needed to be open about my biggest struggle in loving my story line. So I am, even though I can tell I'm twitching as I'm writing this right now.

So me...the hardest area of loving my story line definitely comes in the area of romantic relationships. I'm aware that I've been extremely blessed with good health, an amazing career, fantastic friends, a loving family, and so much more. I have an incredible amount to be grateful for, and I am. But I honestly never had written into my story line that I wouldn't be married by this point in my life. In my "perfect plan" at this age, I would not only be married but also have some kiddos.

I know I'm not alone in the aloneness. Individuals, at least in the United States, are getting married older and having children older. Plus, when you add on the impact of divorce, that leaves a much, much higher percentage of the adult population flying solo than ever before. Even when Adam was in perfect relationship with God, God said that it wasn't good for man to be alone. So this isn't our natural best state.

Yes, we need to find our ultimate source of love and security in God. But scientific research shows that God literally biologically programed us to also connect with someone special. Here's how this truth is explained in *Attached. The New Science of Adult Attachment and How It Can Help You Find—and Keep—Love*:

> When two people form an intimate relationship, they regulate each other's psychological and emotional well-being.... It turns out that the ability to step into the world on our own often stems from the knowledge that there is someone beside us whom we can count on—this is the "dependency paradox." The logic of this paradox is hard to follow at first. How can we act more independent by being thoroughly dependent on someone else? If we had to describe the basic premise of adult attachment in one sentence, it would be: If you want to take the road to independence and happiness, find the right person to depend on and travel down it with that person.[36]

So what do you do when, like me, you find yourself in a situation that you never dreamed that you'd be in, you don't want

---

[36] Amir Levine, MD, and Rachel S. F. Heller, MA, *Attached. The New Science of Adult Attachment and How It Can Help You Find—and Keep—Love* (New York: Jeremy P. Tarcher/Penguin, 2011), 27, 29.

to be in, you know violates your natural biological design, and you feel pretty powerless to change? Sure, you can date plenty of people and be in relationships, but marriage is a gift. (Remember that, all you married people—cherish your spouse.) You can't make it happen. God just decides. Believe me, if one could, I would have figured out a way to make it happen by now. I'm a high achiever.

I don't have the perfect answer to this question of how to be in a place of ongoing disappointment and still trust in God's goodness. (In my case, it's with relationships, but in your case, it could be whatever difficulty is hardest for you right now.) It's an ongoing choice and honestly a struggle that I need to continually bring before the Lord. But I do know that the best place to start is with honesty with God. Gut-wrenching, brutal honesty. Raw emotion. Unvarnished.

If you're not honest with God about how you're hurt, sad, upset, angry, don't trust Him, don't have faith, and hate what He's doing, you'll end up with walls between you and God. I know, I've tried the pretty-Christian-face approach. It doesn't make you feel any better really, and it just pushes God away because you have no authentic connection. You must have openness, honesty, and vulnerability in your communication for trust and intimacy to grow and deepen with anyone, including God. It's OK to come to God when you are struggling with a really bad attitude. That's usually the time when you *most* need His help.

Plus, it's important to admit what's really going on inside so you don't end up trying to covertly force whatever you want to happen in your life because you don't trust that God's taking care of it. Sometimes, God will completely block your efforts when you do this. Other times, God will let you have less than

His best because you're fighting Him so hard and He gives you free will. But when you do get what you want "your way," be it a relationship, a job, a possession, or anything else, you hide it from God because you're afraid that He'll take it away. And whatever you got doesn't end up really satisfying you or feeling like you had hoped it would because it's an idol that you're putting ahead of God instead of a gift that helps you to rejoice in God all the more.

Believe me. This is a bad life choice. Stop it. I've tried this strategy more times than I would like to admit. God always wins, so you might as well give up now.

Be honest. Be brave. Tell it to God like it is. He can handle it. He has never gotten mad at me for telling Him my struggles and fears and even anger in a raw way. My cries to God usually happen most intensely when I'm fresh from a breakup that either I or the other person in the relationship has decided to let go. No matter what the situation around the breakup, God always draws me close and wraps me up in His arms. A lot of times, He also strokes my hair and tells me, "I know, E. I'm so sorry that it's so hard." No condemnation. No telling me I shouldn't have dated the person anyway. No chastising me for ways in which I got offtrack in the

> *When tempted, no one should say, "God is tempting me." For God cannot be tempted by evil, nor does he tempt anyone; but each person is tempted when they are dragged away by their own evil desire and enticed. Then, after desire has conceived, it gives birth to sin; and sin, when it is full-grown, gives birth to death.*
>
> *Don't be deceived, my dear brothers and sisters. Every good and perfect gift is from above, coming down from the Father of the heavenly lights, who does not change like shifting shadows.*
>
> JAMES 1:13-17

relationship. No invalidating my pain because He knows that so much better is on the way. Just tenderness.

A tear rolled down my cheek right now thinking about God's immense compassion for me in my struggle and weakness. Even when I know I'm totally undeserving of compassion and acting irrational and ungrateful (let's admit it—we all have our moments), He still loves me and wants nothing more than to be with me in the mess. Knowing this makes the anger go. The entitlement go. The bitterness go. And all that is left is pure love. When I get to the point where I can recognize that I've epically failed in my efforts to *earn love*, I can finally just *receive love*.

When we stay close to Him, then the peace comes, then the faith comes, then the trust comes. It just happens from God's presence. Knowing God is with us—that we never have been and never will be alone—transforms hard times from experiences of trauma to ones of growth and healing. In our greatest brokenness, God desires to do His greatest work of redemption.

Then once we've restored that place of relationship with God, then we can get into telling ourselves the truth of God's Word about loving our story line. But before, it's just really not helpful. It feels fake, forced, and invalidating of our pain. If you're prone to depression, you may need to give yourself a time limit on having a pity party. But for me, I find my heart knows when it's time to make the shift. It's important I give myself time to get upset and feel whatever I feel. Then I can authentically and effectively get into a more holy mental space.

When it's time to make the shift into more positive thinking about my story line, it really helps to regain some perspective about the truth of my life and life journey as a Christian. First of all, my life isn't my own. I'm God's, and my goal needs to be alignment with His will:

> Then he called the crowd to him along with his disciples and said: "Whoever wants to be my disciple must deny themselves and take up their cross and follow me. For whoever wants to save their life will lose it, but whoever loses their life for me and for the gospel will save it. What good is it for someone to gain the whole world, yet forfeit their soul? Or what can anyone give in exchange for their soul?"
>
> (Mark 8:34–37)

In light of where I'm at in life, sure there are things that I can do to be my best self, get out, do online dating, be open to introductions, etc. But ultimately my life is not my own. I'm God's. If He's decided that I'm going to get married in one year, five years, ten years, etc., it's His choice. I may think His choice stinks and not like it one bit, but it is His choice. (Kind of like Abraham and Sarah had their share of frustrations with waiting decades for Isaac, and Joseph had a less-than-smooth life journey. God decides.) I must come out of agreement with the lies that I'm a failure, a loser, and worthy of pity. I must choose to believe the truth that I'm beloved, precious, blessed, cared for, provided for, chosen, and protected regardless of my relationship status, right here and right now. I must also come out of agreement with the lies that God doesn't see, doesn't care, and isn't actively working on my behalf to take care of me and fulfill the desires of my heart. I'll lead my best life when I come to a place of acceptance, peace, and even joy about God's will for my life instead of resisting it.

When I'm really struggling, I find it's helpful to say out loud, "God, I accept your will for me today. I accept that you have decided that it's not yet the right time for me to be in a relationship. Please show me how you want me to use the time I have today. Please grow and mature me into the woman who is ready for all you have prepared for me."

This intentional acceptance and submission to the Lord's plans and process calms my soul and eliminates any tension between me and God. I also find that it takes me from obsessive focus on the one thing in my life that is not how I want it to a broader view of my life. This more expansive perspective makes me intensely grateful for all the good that I have in my life right now and all the ways God has and is answering my prayers in the present.

Pastor Tim Dilena did an incredibly encouraging and convicting talk at Times Square Church on "What's In Between Ask and Receive." You can watch the full sermon here: https://www .youtube.com/watch?v=ZTkx_WBFNsE.[37]

But here are a few of my favorite quotes from the message that could give you perspective on your story line:

"God will never give you a position or possession that you will sabotage with your immaturity."
"There's always a journey to get you ready for the thing you asked."

---

[37] "January 29, 2017 - Tim Dilena - What's In Between Ask and Receive," YouTube video, 49:36, posted by Times Square Church, accessed May 1, 2017, https:// www.youtube.com/watch?v=ZTkx_WBFNsE.

"When you're faithful in the little, God will make you ruler of much."

"Delay is not denial."

"Delay is not God's inability but my immaturity, which God will solve on the journey."

"When you pray one thing, God has to do ten thousand things."

"While you're complaining, God's coordinating."

There's beauty in every life path and reasons for gratitude and joy in every moment.

I like how life coach Brenda Stanton put it in her post "How Fear Rules Your Life":

The biggest realization I had going into this year is when my own coach said to me: "You're trying to create your life and it's not yours to create." Whoa—that hit me between the eyes—because I know that is the Truth.

The Truth is: your destiny isn't something you can conjure up in your mind. Your destiny is what your soul has already agreed to—and it's pulling you towards it each day. Your job is to listen, trust and be present in the moment in order to hear its guidance.

But, if you allow fear to be in charge, then you'll always be afraid of what you've always been afraid of—and then nothing can change. In other words, as someone said to me, as long as your reality has to go off what fear says, fear will win.

A different reality is trying to choose you, your choice is, will you allow it or stop it? One is letting your soul guide you and the other is letting fear be in charge. Which will you choose? Remember, choose yourself first and you'll always make the best choice.[38]

As one of my very wise coaching clients put it, "There's no part of life that isn't part of the sacred path."

For someone who built a career around teaching people how to be more "in control," this way of thinking and being used to trigger both a sense of exhilarating relief and sheer terror. What do you mean I'm not in control of my destiny? How do I get to where I want to go?

It's been a process. But I've learned that life can be much more effortless than I ever imagined. When I say no to everything that doesn't feel in alignment and then focus wholeheartedly on what is in alignment, far more results happen with far less effort, and I'm my true self. That's God's best.

■　■　■

So if we're not supposed to try to make our plans happen, what are we supposed to focus on? Well, the short answer is God. Psalm 27:4 puts it this way:

One thing I have asked from the LORD, that I shall seek:
That I may dwell in the house of the LORD all the days
of my life,
to behold the beauty of the LORD
and to meditate in His temple.

(NASB)

---

[38] "How Fear Rules Your Life," accessed January 17, 2017, http://brendastanton.com/fear-rules-life.

Some people are called to take this very literally. At the International House of Prayer Missions Base of Kansas City, there are people who worship the Lord as their full-time vocation. At this house of worship, there has literally been 24/7 worship of the Lord since September 19, 1999.

But not all of us are called to live a life of missions work in that way, so what about us? We should commit ourselves to what God has called us to do at any particular time.

Right now in general for all of us that means looking to have love and connection flow between ourselves, God, and everyone we encounter. God didn't command us just to love our significant other or children or close friends. He calls us to love Him and to love our neighbor—meaning everyone He puts in our path—as ourselves. To do this, I've tried to be more conscious to slow down and be open. That means when I'm working on the manuscript for this book at a coffee shop, being open to conversation when it happens and seeing it as a gift, not a distraction. Or when I check out at a store, being present to the person helping me. Or when I have a random call come in from a friend or family member, appreciating that opportunity to connect even when I wasn't expecting it.

For me specifically, at this point in my life, it means writing this book and sharing God's light

> On one occasion an expert in the law stood up to test Jesus. "Teacher," he asked, "what must I do to inherit eternal life?"
>
> "What is written in the Law?" he replied. "How do you read it?"
>
> He answered, "'Love the Lord your God with all your heart and with all your soul and with all your strength and with all your mind'; and, 'Love your neighbor as yourself.'"
>
> "You have answered correctly," Jesus replied. "Do this and you will live."
>
> LUKE 10:25-28

and love in a bigger way through my work. Doing some sort of public ministry where I shared about my faith is not something I ever dreamed I would be doing. But it's what God has for me now. I have to trust that as I do what God wants, He will fulfill the desires of my heart in His perfect way and time for getting married and having children and everything else I could possibly want or need and more.

God will do this for me not because I deserve it or because He owes me something for good behavior. God already has given me more than I could ever deserve in Jesus. But God will come through on His promises to me because He is the perfect Father, He loves me, delights in giving me good gifts, and He is always faithful to His word. And I have to remember that my hope, trust, love, and life must always be ultimately fulfilled in God, not a person or people. I'm blessed now, and I will be blessed in my future circumstances because the Lord is with me. No moment with God is ever a waste. It's a gift.

> Take delight in the LORD, and he will give you the desires of your heart.
>
> PSALM 37:4
>
> The king rejoices in your strength, LORD.
> How great is his joy in the victories you give!
> You have granted him his heart's desire
> and have not withheld the request of his lips.
>
> PSALM 21:1-2

In loving our story line, we must recognize that our lives aren't our own, that we need to seek God's kingdom first and be in His will. Then, finally, we need to have a simple trust in God's goodness. That God is good and loving to us in the present, even when it doesn't feel like goodness. Also that even if we never see something good out of the pain on earth, that there will be redemption in heaven. As it says in James 1:2–4:

Consider it a sheer gift, friends, when tests and challenges
come at you from all sides. You know that under pressure,
your faith-life is forced into the open and shows its true
colors. So don't try to get out of anything prematurely.
Let it do its work so you become mature and well-
developed, not deficient in any way.

(MSG)

And in 2 Corinthians 4:16–18 we're encouraged in this manner:

Therefore we do not lose heart. Though outwardly we
are wasting away, yet inwardly we are being renewed
day by day. For our light and momentary troubles are
achieving for us an eternal glory that far outweighs them
all. So we fix our eyes not on what is seen, but on what
is unseen, since what is seen is temporary, but what is
unseen is eternal.

Melissa Helser is one of my favorite worship artists, and she
did an interview published on CBN.com about her struggle with
psoriatic arthritis.[39] This interview includes her testimony about
how God miraculously healed her, the affliction came back, and
how she has experienced healing again but up until this point
not full recovery. You can view it here: https://www.youtube
.com/watch?v=A2GgT5ayFik.

I love how Melissa emphasizes that she still trusts God is
good even when she can't see what He's doing or why He doesn't
miraculously heal her as she knows and believes He could. I

---

[39] "Breaking from Bitterness to Release Healing," YouTube video, 6:36, posted
by the Official 700 Club, accessed January 17, 2017, https://www.youtube
.com/watch?v=A2GgT5ayFik.

believe that as we face whatever is part of our story line, including a past littered with disappointment and a future unknown, that God wants us to cling to the truth of His unchanging character again and again. That He is good. That He is faithful. That He is loving. That He wants you and me to continue to hope. To believe in His promises more than our experiences. As Graham Cooke would say, to "stay joyfully vulnerable to God's goodness."[40] Not grasping for what we want when we want it and yet also not closing ourselves off from God's best: all that He wants to and can do in our lives both now and in heaven.

The devil is a liar, and he will constantly try to tell you that God doesn't hear, see, or care, that you are a failure and hopeless, and that nothing will ever change. But as my very wise Divine Time Management coaching client and friend Jim Evans says, "I always like to remember that the enemy only speaks lies, and there is no truth in him at all." Basically whatever the devil tells you, think the opposite. In doing so, you'll turn all curses into mighty blessings and enter into God's best.

This song, written by Edward Francis Conlin III, a man who has devoted his life to the Lord, I believe best describes the perspective that leads to love of our story line, ourselves, and our God:

Prayer of Augustine

O Beauty ancient, O Beauty so new
Late have I loved Thee and feebly yet do.
Though You were with me, I was not with You.
Then You shone Your face and I was blind no more

---

[40] "Joyfully Vulnerable to God's Goodness Graham Cooke 5 30 10," YouTube video, 1:07:26, posted by elvenranger04, accessed on January 17, 2017, https://www.youtube.com/watch?v=5b7ItLQO8zg.

My heart searches restlessly and finds no rest 'till it rests in Thee.
O Seeker You sought for me, Your love has found me;
I am taken by Thee.
I sought this world and chased its finer things,
Yet were these not in You, they would not have been.
My ceaseless longing hid the deeper truth,
In all my desirings, I was desiring You.

My heart searches restlessly and finds no rest 'till it rests in Thee.
O Seeker You sought for me, Your love has found me;
I am taken by Thee.
Lord, in my deafness You cried out to me.
I drew my breath and now Your fragrance I breathe
O Fount of Life, You are forever the same;
O Fire of Love, come set me aflame.

My heart searches restlessly and finds no rest 'till it rests in Thee.
O Seeker You sought for me, Your love has found me;
I am taken by Thee.[41]

Reflection Exercise: EMBRACING OUR LIMITS

Despite some common beliefs in various church settings, God doesn't despise the fact that we're not machines. He loves it and created us that way on purpose.

God didn't have to make us with the need for sleep, for food, for rest, for connection. But He chose to. I believe He chose to do that first and foremost to keep us dependent on His loving care.

---

[41] Edward Francis Conlin III, "Prayer of Augustine," accessed on January 17, 2017, http://www.swordofthespirit.net/bulwark/february2014p17.htm.

Reasonable self-care: wanting time to sleep, eat, do physical activity, and time for mental, emotional, and spiritual renewal—even a few minutes a day, isn't selfish. It's simply being human.

As you think about how to incorporate more self-care into your life, I want to encourage you to ask God: "How did you make me? How did you design me to best function?" Then think through ways that you could make simple shifts to incorporate more of what gives you life into your life.

If you're a little stumped and don't even know what you want, here's a starting point based on research from the American Psychological Association on stress-relief strategies that work best. They include "exercising or playing sports, praying or attending a religious service, reading, listening to music, spending time with friends or family, getting a massage, going outside for a walk, meditating or doing yoga, and spending time with a creative hobby. (The least effective strategies are gambling, shopping, smoking, drinking, eating, playing video games, surfing the Internet, and watching TV or movies for more than two hours.)"[42]

So for example, you could:

- Go on a walk after dinner instead of only watching TV
- Turn off the radio on the way to work so you can pray as you drive
- Make it a priority to meet a friend for lunch once a week
- Spend time in nature such as by water or in the woods

---

[42] Kelly McGonigal, PhD, *The Willpower Instinct: How Self-Control Works, Why It Matters, and What You Can Do to Get More of It* (New York: Avery, 2012), 137.

Exactly what you do will depend on your individual needs. But taking small steps to get rejuvenated can lead to massive increases in the fruits of the Spirit and your ability to love God and others.

God's best,

Elizabeth

> *It is vain for you to rise up early,*
> *To retire late,*
> *To eat the bread of painful labors;*
> *For He gives to His beloved even in his sleep.*
>
> PSALM 127:2 NASB

A Few Final Thoughts

But he gives us more grace. That is why Scripture says:
"God opposes the proud
but shows favor to the humble."
Submit yourselves, then, to God. Resist the devil, and he will flee
from you. Come near to God and he will come near to you....
Humble yourselves before the Lord, and he will lift you up.

JAMES 4:6–8a, 10

I often wondered why God picked me to write this book on letting go of control. The best I can tell, He has a really good sense of humor.

I started out feeling pretty good about my credentials. But through the process of writing *Divine Time Management*, I've realized how completely unqualified I was to write it: a type A personality, a planner, a high achiever, a go-getter, and a time management coach, for goodness' sake! I thought I had mastered the art of being in control for most of my life and was proud of it. And here I am writing about how to do the opposite of what I've spent most of my years doing and teaching others to do.

The best I can tell, it all comes down to one simple word: grace.

My heart's desire is that in reading this book that you've experienced what I've experienced in writing it: encouragement, inspiration, insight, deep conviction, and most important hope that you can live a life full of joy trusting in God's loving plans for you.

Because ultimately this isn't all about me or you or our shortcomings, it's about the perfect grace, mercy, power, and love of the Father expressed through the life, death, and resurrection of His Son Jesus Christ.

When we enter into divine time management by replacing control with trust, love, and alignment with God, we will absolutely experience God's best.

What exactly is God's best for your life and my life? I really don't know. I can't predict it or put it in a box, because God's infinitely wise and oh so creative.

But what I do know is that God is good, that He has good plans for you, that He will work everything for good in your life, and that He can do far more than you could ask or think or imagine. My prayer for you is that you will align your time with God's will and experience these truths on a deeper, richer level each and every day.

Your role in the process is to put trust in God at the center, love your true identity, and stay in alignment with God. So simple and yet so difficult at the same time. But with God's help, you can do it!

And, oh yeah…watch out for miracles and tell me about them! You can contact me through my website at www.RealLifeE.com.

Much love and every blessing,

Elizabeth Grace

Now unto Him that is able to do exceeding abundantly above all that we ask or think, according to the power that worketh in us, unto Him be glory in the church by Christ Jesus throughout all ages, world without end. Amen.

EPHESIANS 3:20–21 KJ21

In Gratitude

I'm deeply grateful for the opportunity to write this book and to share it with the world. Thank you to my book agent, Giles Anderson, for believing in the concept and to Virginia Bhashkar, Christina Boys, and Joey Paul, editors at FaithWords, for partnering with me in bringing the book to fruition. Thank you also to Sara Timm and Jim Evans, invaluable members of the Real Life E team who contribute amazing work and even more amazing prayer support and encouragement along the way.

Also, I have incredible gratitude toward my Divine Time Management group coaching members, time management coaching clients, newsletter subscribers, and book readers. I feel like I learn as much from you as I teach. I appreciate the opportunity to be on the journey with you and am inspired by your joy, trust, and faith in the Lord in the midst of life's triumphs and struggles.

Many thanks to all of the churches and Christian groups that have been part of my faith journey. Every group I've been in and person I've learned from has contributed to who I am today. I'm blessed and enriched by the company of so many believers who love and honor the Lord so well.

Yeah for my great family and friends! There are so many people who have encouraged me on my journey. Of course, thanks to my mom, dad, and my siblings and my many friends, cheerleaders, prayer warriors, and book-writing buddies. I really appreciate all of the support you've shown me and know this wouldn't be possible without you.

And last, and most important, thank you, God. I'm honored to share about You and Your heart in a deeper way with others through this book. In myself, I know I'm unworthy. But I thank You that, through Christ, I'm made completely worthy for the service You have for me. My prayer is that this work will make Your heart glad, draw many into a deeper relationship with You, and bring great healing, joy, and freedom. May Your kingdom come and Your will be done on earth as it is in heaven. Amen.

"For I know the plans I have for you," declares the LORD, *"plans to prosper you and not to harm you, plans to give you hope and a future."*

JEREMIAH 29:11

About the Author

ELIZABETH GRACE SAUNDERS is the founder and CEO of Real Life E, a time management coaching company that has helped clients on six continents to go from feeling guilty, overwhelmed, and frustrated to feeling peaceful, confident, and accomplished. She is an expert on achieving more success with less stress. She has spoken to thousands of individuals, including speaking after Steve Forbes at a business retreat. Real Life E also encourages Christians to align themselves with God's heart through a Divine Time Management group coaching program.

Elizabeth has appeared as an expert in numerous offline and online media outlets including *Forbes*, *Harvard Business Review*, *Fast Company*, *TIME*, *Mashable*, *London Evening Standard*, *Woman's Day*, *Inc.*, *Design*Sponge*, and *Huffington Post*. She has appeared on CBS, ABC, NBC, and Fox. Most important, she's a beloved daughter of God saved by grace.

For exclusive time investment material, go to www.Schedule Makeover.com. You can also find more articles, resources, and information on Elizabeth's coaching and speaking at www.Real LifeE.com and on Divine Time Management group coaching at www.DivineTimeManagement.com.